Let Go of the Guilt

STOP BEATING YOURSELF UP
AND TAKE BACK YOUR JOY

VALORIE BURTON

W PUBLISHING GROUP

AN IMPRINT OF THOMAS NELSON

Published in Nashville, Tennessee, by W Publishing, an imprint of Thomas Nelson.

The author is represented by Alive Literary Agency, 7680 Goddard Street, Suite 200, Colorado Springs, Colorado 80920, www.aliveliterary.com.

Thomas Nelson titles may be purchased in bulk for educational, business, fundraising, or sales promotional use. For information, please email SpecialMarkets@ ThomasNelson.com.

Scripture quotations marked KJV are taken from the King James Version. Public domain.

Scripture quotations marked THE MESSAGE are from *The Message*. Copyright © by Eugene H. Peterson 1993, 1994, 1995, 1996, 2000, 2001, 2002. Used by permission of NavPress. All rights reserved. Represented by Tyndale House Publishers, Inc.

Scripture quotations marked NIV are from the Holy Bible, New International Version®, NIV®. Copyright © 1973, 1978, 1984, 2011 by Biblica, Inc.® Used by permission of Zondervan. All rights reserved worldwide. www.Zondervan.com. The "NIV" and "New International Version" are trademarks registered in the United States Patent and Trademark Office by Biblica, Inc.®

Any internet addresses, phone numbers, or company or product information printed in this book are offered as a resource and are not intended in any way to be or to imply an endorsement by Thomas Nelson, nor does Thomas Nelson vouch for the existence, content, or services of these sites, phone numbers, companies, or products beyond the life of this book.

ISBN 978-0-7852-2022-0 (eBook)
ISBN 978-0-7852-2021-3 (TP)

Library of Congress Cataloging-in-Publication Data

Library of Congress Control Number: 2020937458

Printed in the United States of America

20 21 22 23 24   LSC   10 9 8 7 6 5 4 3 2

May these words be exactly what you need to let go of the guilt and embrace the freedom, truth, and joy you deserve and desire.

Contents

CONTENTS

Introduction: Why Did You Do That?

How Guilt Can Drive Your Decisions

I don't know what sort of guilt led you to pick up this book, but know this: you are not alone. I wrote this book for you, but the truths and steps I share in the coming pages also helped me.

Pangs of guilt, whether I was *actually* guilty of something or not, have left me anxious and worried throughout my life. Even worse, guilt has nudged me to do things I otherwise knew made no sense—as I did one morning not long after I started this project. Perhaps it happened for your entertainment, but it is a prime example of how guilt squeezes its way into our lives and hijacks our emotions and our choices.

It was a Wednesday around 6:55 a.m., and my family and I were making good time. In fact, we were a few minutes ahead of schedule. My five-year-old son, Alex, was dressed and happy and had his teeth brushed, bed made, and shoes on. By this point, midway through the school year, I had given up on insisting my son eat breakfast at the table. He doesn't want eggs or toast. But I'd found a new way to entice him to eat his Cheerios. I bagged his cereal in a plastic zip bag and poured him a cup of milk with a snap-on cover so he could drink it in the car. With the reward of a few minutes of games on my phone, he'd eat quickly on the way to the bus stop. Voilà! It was an easier and faster option than trying to make him sit down and eat this early in the morning. It certainly wasn't the way my mom fed me breakfast growing up, but it worked.

Just as I finished pouring his milk, Alex asked a simple question. "Mommy, can I eat my cereal at the table today?" he asked sweetly.

Now, that may sound reasonable enough. But he eats slowly. And we weren't *that* ahead of schedule.

My guilt-induced response derailed the morning.

"Nope, not today. We don't have time" would have been the obvious answer, but that assumes I responded with logic and common sense. Instead, I was bombarded with a flurry of negative thoughts in rapid secession.

Poor kid.

He has to get up so early in the morning. It's still dark out, for goodness' sake!

He's only five and has to be at the bus stop at 7:15 a.m.

All he wants is to eat breakfast at home, and you're rushing him out the door.

Next came the flashback to my own childhood, when walking into the kitchen each morning was like walking into a full-service Southern diner:

Your mother prepared you a full breakfast—eggs, bacon, grits, toast with butter or grape jelly, depending on your preference, and orange juice. Every. Single. Morning!

She always made sure you ate at the kitchen table when you were his age, and now your own child has to eat cereal in the car.

Alex sat there looking at me, his sweet face patiently waiting for an answer. I looked down at his bag of cereal and recalled a memory that left me feeling even guiltier.

You see, there was only one morning in my entire childhood that my mother gave me cereal for breakfast. I jokingly refer to that morning as the "great cereal experiment"—her one-time attempt to save some time and feed her child what most children eat every morning.

I am in the third grade. I enter the kitchen of our two-bedroom apartment near Frankfurt, West Germany, where my dad is stationed. I sit down at the table, and my mom brings me a bowl of Rice Krispies with milk and way too much sugar, just the way I like it.

I love Rice Krispies. I eat them after school every day as a snack. I don't know why she's letting me have them this morning before my breakfast, but I don't ask any questions because they are yummy. I pretty much inhale them, so she pours me another bowl. I gobble that one up too.

Then she says, "Okay, let's go."

I'm utterly confused. "But I haven't had breakfast yet!" I protest.

"What do you mean?" she asks. "You just had two bowls of cereal."

I look at her in disbelief. "Cereal isn't breakfast. It's a snack."

It's time to leave for school, and my mom looks both perplexed by my reaction and a little guilty because of it.

"There's no time for me to cook now, Valorie," she says. "We've got to go, or you'll be late for school and I'll be late for work."

I grab my book bag and, as we head out the door, I mumble something about how I can't believe she's making me go to school "without breakfast."

That was the one and only morning I ate cereal for breakfast.

Decades later, that morning flashes in my mind. The result?

While my son actually likes cereal for breakfast, my eight-year-old self whispers the refrain *Cereal isn't breakfast*, and I feel a tinge of guilt for giving it to him. Layer that on top of all my other thoughts that morning, and you end up with the answer I gave Alex to his simple question. I knew the logical answer. But *logic* didn't answer Alex. *Guilt* did.

"Sure, pumpkin. We can eat here, but you have to hurry. I wasn't planning on this."

You can guess what happened next: he took his time. I tried to speed him along, but by the time we left the house, I knew it would take a near-miracle to get to the bus stop on time. Alex goes to an independent school across town, and we are lucky enough to have a centrally located bus stop a few minutes from home. But if we don't make the bus stop, it's a forty-minute hike through traffic to get to the school.

My hands clenched the steering wheel, as though that would get us there a little faster. My eyes darted from the clock to the road and back to the clock again. My shoulders tensed; I drove with laser-like focus. As green lights seemed to usher me straight toward the bus stop, it felt like divine orchestration. *Yes! Maybe we can make it after all!*

I held my breath, hoping that perhaps a few kids were still boarding the bus, as I turned the corner into the bus stop parking lot.

Suddenly, the car jolted. *Boom!*

My tire had hit the curb *hard*. Then, in what felt like slow motion, I saw Alex's bus pulling away and heading out of the parking lot.

If I just keep going, I can catch the bus driver before he turns onto the main road, I thought.

I steered back onto the street and kept driving toward the bus, hoping to catch the driver's attention. But I could tell at least one of my tires was flat, my SUV was leaning to one side, and I could hear the punctured rubber flopping against the asphalt with every rotation of the wheel.

"Mommy, I think you should slow down!" Alex advised from the back. We had no choice, actually. We hobbled toward the bus at about ten miles an hour. Thank God the bus driver saw us and stopped. The bus's red stop sign opened up as I jumped out of the car and ran around to the opposite side to help Alex and rush him onto the bus. He made it.

I turned into a parking space and sat in frazzled silence. How did a morning that started out peaceful and ahead of schedule end up with two blown-out tires and Alex nearly missing the bus?

It wasn't simply that I had overestimated how much time we had or that I thought Alex should eat at home. The real culprit was *guilt*. When he asked if he could eat at the kitchen table, the ensuing guilt hijacked my thoughts, then drove my actions. The resulting events cost me peace, more than six hours getting my car towed and fixed, and more than $800 in repairs, all of which could have been avoided if guilt wasn't in the driver's seat. But it was. And that's why you and I are here right now. It's why you were drawn to this book.

Guilt is sneaky. It doesn't just rob you of joy. Even more insidious is the way it can drive decisions and actions that sabotage you before you even realize what's happening. It triggers automatic reactions that can have you apologizing, overcompensating, and beating yourself up with the skill of a heavyweight champion.

Whether it's that voice inside your head reminding you of expectations you haven't lived up to or the mistake you made years ago that you are still paying the price for, the emotion of guilt plays a repeated message: *I am not enough. I am not doing enough. I am not getting it right. I should be doing something more. Something different. Something better. But I am not, so I am going to feel guilty. I'll rehash my shortcomings. And worst of all, I will hold my happiness hostage. I'll dampen it with this broken record of self-criticism.*

In my case, I realized that guilt hadn't just shown up one little morning for one little thing. It was showing up a whole lot of mornings, throughout my day, into my night, and in my relationships with my children, my husband, my friends, my parents, and my employees. It affected my finances and even my spiritual life. And as I raised my awareness of the omnipresence of guilt, I began to see it everywhere—not just in my own life, but in comments from friends, coaching sessions with clients, and comments from women in my audiences. I thought, *Is it just me? Am I imagining that women everywhere are dealing with this too?*

I believe guilt is epidemic among women. I believe guilt is epidemic among *today's* women, who are burdened with more expectations than any generation has ever had, brought on by the greatest breakthrough of opportunities any generation has ever experienced. Guilt isn't going away; it's coming on stronger than ever.

When you let guilt take control, it subconsciously rules your decisions—about relationships, about money, even about what you eat and whether you worship. It keeps you from following your dreams. Leaves you resentful. Makes you love begrudgingly. Pushes away the love you really want.

Guilt drives you to say yes when you want to say no. It fills up your schedule with stuff that isn't purposeful while stealing time from the things that are. And it nags. It weighs heavily.

Rooted in past experiences and unexamined expectations, my guilt drove my actions in answer to Alex's request that morning. See how quickly feelings of guilt can derail our best intentions? As you move through these pages, I'll show you how to intentionally choose your thoughts and let go of the ones that create false guilt that can take over your life.

What's at Stake

If you let guilt answer the little questions of life for you, then you are prone to letting guilt answer the big questions as well. Sometimes the consequences aren't as easy to overcome as a nearly missed bus and a couple of busted tires. The issues are bigger and the consequences more dire.

Over the years I've not only worked through my own struggles with guilt but also coached hundreds of individuals through theirs. Nicole confessed she married her now ex-husband out of guilt. Sherri wouldn't ask for a raise out of guilt that she was being selfish. Kim felt obligated to keep volunteering at her cousin's nonprofit because her cousin had helped her get on her feet during a rough period more than a decade ago. And Megan admitted, "Guilt informs most of my day, even though I don't consciously think about it." She felt guilty about not sticking to her diet, guilty about not exercising more, guilty about her spouse moving across the country for her and leaving his family behind—even though it was his idea.

What's at stake when we don't let go of the guilt? We give up freedom. We give up joy. We give up peace.

Guilt shows up in many ways. Maybe some of these look familiar to you:

- Beating yourself up for past choices, mistakes, and imperfections
- Feeling as though you can never do enough
- Having very little, if any, peace or joy in your relationships
- Feeling stressed, resentful, or devalued in your relationships
- Making less money than you deserve
- Paying more than you have to
- Saying yes when the best answer is no
- Allowing others to guilt trip you
- Letting others repeatedly overstep boundaries
- Downplaying successes to make others feel comfortable
- Ending up in codependent relationships
- Pretending as though dysfunctional behavior is normal
- Not speaking up when you need and want to
- Making decisions out of guilt and obligation
- Feeling indebted indefinitely to someone who did you a favor
- Second-guessing yourself
- Feeling dread as your norm

Letting guilt take the driver's seat can leave you resentful and overworked, manipulated and taken advantage of, and bruised from beating yourself up for falling short of your expectations—expectations that are sometimes impossible to meet.

A moment that could be savored and enjoyed suddenly becomes stressful and filled with negative emotions. My morning with Alex, which could have been lovely and unrushed, turned into an unnecessary mess. But that's just the tip of the iceberg.

In this book, I share real stories that help you see the myriad ways guilt can control the direction of your life if you allow it to. Whether you're dealing with past choices that haunt you or the successes you downplay because of guilt that others close to you don't share the same good fortune, the goal of this book is to help you see the problem and then conquer it. You don't have to be controlled by guilt.

If you picked up this book, I know you have a deep longing to lift the burden of guilt off your shoulders, to be fully happy, and to untangle yourself from the grip of guilt trips and emotional manipulation. I wish I were sitting there with you right now, but know that, as I write these words, my sincere desire is to help you have a breakthrough.

I want for you what I wanted for myself—to stop feeling guilty about things you haven't done wrong. I want you to have the strength to resist guilt trips. I want you to tell the truth and know it's possible to be honest about how you feel in ways that honor the people you care about. I want you to have the joy you deserve without dampening that joy with unnecessary worry, fear, and anxiety.

> I want for you what I wanted for myself—to stop feeling guilty about things you haven't done wrong.

Taking steps to free yourself from excessive guilt is really about freeing yourself to live the life God created you for. It is about your willingness and desire to be whole and healthy, to call out lies with truth, and to be bold enough to set and honor your personal boundaries. If you are willing to do the work of pushing through your fears and trusting there's a better way to live, I believe with all my heart that you will have a breakthrough.

In the instances when you really are guilty of something, I want you to boldly look for the message that guilt can send. Because when we address guilt with truth, we are free to embrace the changes we need to make in our own lives, to align our values with our everyday actions, and begin the work of forgiveness that frees us.

Who I Am

When I set out to write a book about guilt, I didn't realize that this subject can feel deeply sad to talk about. It can conjure up anxiety and all sorts of negative emotions.

I am a life coach. My background is in applied positive psychology, and my favorite research is around positive emotions, not negative ones. So after I began to delve deeper into the subject, I realized that I wasn't really prepared. I asked myself, *What's your intention? What can you offer from your perspective that will uniquely empower readers? Is there something specific that coaching and positive psychology offer that can get people unstuck from guilt?* The answers to these questions excited me and filled me with desire to help you gain joy and freedom.

Many books on guilt feel very heavy. I think because of this, some of us avoid the subject altogether, even though it's stealing our joy. That's why I take an intentionally uplifting approach to overcoming guilt. My mission is inspiring women to live more fulfilling lives. But living a fulfilling life is not just about finding positive emotions; it is also about understanding the negative emotions that prevent more positive ones. It is important to understand that negative emotions are not bad things. They can teach us. And we have to learn not to simply push negative emotions away but to allow them to become a part of our lived experience—not to be avoided but instead be managed and even transformed.

I'm going to coach you through a process that will enable you to let go of the guilt. Just as important, I'll help you understand the dynamics that will make it easier for you to let go.

How Coaching Works

Coaching is a process that helps you move from where you are to where you want to be, and to navigate all of the obstacles, fears, and opportunities that arise along the way. I've been a life coach since 2002. In 2009, I founded Coaching and Positive Psychology (CaPP) Institute, which has trained personal and executive coaches from every state in the United States and more than fifteen countries on six continents. I believe in coaching because it works. It has worked in my life, and I have seen how it transforms the lives of others—giving them clarity about their vision and values, their purpose and possibilities. It helps them find answers to the dilemmas they face and empowers them with the confidence to do things they've dreamed of.

Good coaching creates powerful breakthroughs. For this book, I have developed a process for letting go of guilt by delivering the concept of coaching in writing. I have used this process myself, and I have used it to help create breakthroughs for clients and women whose stories I share in these pages. These breakthroughs empowered them to finally let go of guilt that has plagued them for years, and in some cases, decades. Just as important, letting go of guilt changed how they make decisions, communicate, and live their everyday lives.

Of course, we are doing this in book form, and I am inviting you to coach yourself using the powerful questions (or "PQs" as I like to call them) I give you. I suggest you journal through your answers. Take out a notebook or open up your computer, or even dictate into the notes app on your phone. Writing out your thoughts is much more powerful than trying to sort through them quietly in your head. Often, we have so many thoughts at once that we lose some of them. And the ones we lose can be important pieces of the puzzle. Without keeping track of them, we lose that one piece that would help us make sense of it all. So while it's tempting to just read and think, I encourage you to read, think, and write down what you think if you really want to get the answers you need.

Over the years, when I have used these techniques to help clients have breakthroughs and let go of guilt, I've grown more flexible with the order in which I ask questions. I have discovered this is not a rigid process but rather a fluid one. Notice the answers that tug at you, and delve deeper into the reasons for that. That is where you will begin to have powerful aha moments and insights.

If you are ready to be free of guilt and make changes that can transform your life and relationships, you are in the right place. I'm excited to serve as your coach. All I ask is that you be honest as I challenge you with questions that can shift your perspective, give you clarity and courage, and equip you with a plan of action.

Over and over, I've heard the same reaction almost verbatim after I guide others through this process: "I feel like a weight has been lifted off of me. I feel so much lighter."

Guilt is heavy. It weighs you down. But it doesn't have to be this way. It's time to let it go. Allow me to be your coach. Let's get started!

What Are You Feeling Guilty About?

The First Step to Conquering
Your Guilt Is Naming It

- What are the three truths of guilt?
- Do you have authentic guilt or false guilt?
- What's on your guilt list?

I had just finished a keynote message to a group of three thousand women leaders from hundreds of top companies around the world, and I felt energized as I walked off the stage. I had talked about how successful women think differently, a topic at the core of my purpose. But the organization had also requested that I do a breakout session—a coaching workshop on something that wasn't my typical topic. "Work-Life Balance for Working Parents," they called it.

While I had written about time and busyness, I didn't consider myself an expert on parenting or working parenthood. I was forty before I became a parent. I was still trying to navigate these waters, learning to write books and travel and run a business with young kids at home. It wasn't easy. So as I began the breakout session, I decided to be totally transparent.

"Listen," I began. "I'm a life coach. So I am going to share some powerful questions to coach you to find answers that will help you create some harmony between the demands of your work life and your personal life. But let me be honest," I continued almost apologetically. "Even when I implement my own answers, I sometimes feel an underlying conflict: *guilt*. Anyone else here ever feel guilty?"

The reaction was immediate: Moans. Eye rolls. Heads nodding up and down. As the women looked around the room at each other and saw the collective reaction, hands began to fly up. I had struck a nerve, and they wanted to talk about it. Each woman I called on gave voice to her guilt. And the nods and groans of the other women around the room confirmed they were not alone in their feelings. Their dilemmas were varied, but the feeling of guilt was the same.

"Every month I travel one week for work," a first-time mom explained. "I leave my nine-month-old baby. My husband takes good care of her, and I was doing fine with our arrangement at first, but all the questions and comments from other women constantly get to me. The little remarks are what get me—the passive-aggressive stuff like, 'I don't know how you're away from home so much. I couldn't do it.' At work I keep my guilt to myself because I'm afraid it'll jeopardize my opportunity for promotion."

"I feel guilty I'm not there more for my parents," another woman said, sounding both ashamed and exhausted. "They live about 150 miles away. They're getting older, and I should visit them more, but I'm too busy. What kind of daughter is too busy to visit her aging parents?"

"I was the first in my family to graduate from college, so

sometimes I feel guilty about my success," a woman in her early thirties chimed in. "I'm the go-to person whenever anyone in my family has a problem, especially a financial one. And because I don't have children, it's like everyone thinks I should help all the time. I feel guilty because they're struggling, but if I keep bailing them out, I will never make progress on my own goals."

"I feel guilty that I didn't prepare my kids to 'launch,'" a fiftysomething executive said with a wistful chuckle, referring to her two adult children living at home. "I did too much for them. I think I felt guilty about them having to deal with being in a single-parent household, so I went easy on them. I am driven and responsible, but somehow I didn't pass that on to my kids like I should have."

As each woman shared her story, others nodded in understanding. I, too, struggled with guilt. Long before I ever had mom guilt, I had plain old guilt-guilt. My guilt list was long: Life coach guilt. Divorce guilt. Procrastination guilt. Could-have-done-it-better guilt. Spending guilt. Boss guilt. Ambition guilt.

I chose a profession in which my life is a laboratory for the work I do. So I told myself that if I was going to be coaching others and writing books, I shouldn't have any struggles; I'm the one who helps others overcome theirs. From clutter and procrastination to relationship challenges and money, I was supposed to have all the answers—which meant that I didn't allow myself much grace to be human.

Of course, this type of guilt isn't unique to life coaching and psychology professionals; we see it in the nurse who doesn't eat healthy, the accountant who messes up her own finances, or the stay-at-home mom who feels she never measures up to mother-hood perfection. We can beat ourselves up even more when we don't measure up to ideals.

Guilt robs you of your rights. As a life coach, I told myself I didn't have the right to not know the answers to a challenge. I also felt I'd lost the right to have drive; I sometimes felt guilty about having big goals. Even though I felt my goals were purpose driven, there were days doubts crept in and I questioned whether the goals were selfish. So when these women started sharing their guilt lists, I nodded right along with them.

It wasn't until that day, in that room, that I realized just how strongly other women seemed to feel similar feelings, and that we are dealing with a wide array of what I like to call *guilt dilemmas*—the situations in our lives that trigger feelings of guilt. To test whether the feedback at the workshop was just a fluke, I started mentioning guilt at speaking engagements and in coaching sessions and everyday conversations. Sure enough, each time I'd mention guilt, the response was a heavy sigh.

I wanted to hear more perspectives, so I surveyed more than five hundred women on the topic. What were they feeling guilty about exactly? Here is just a glimpse of what some had to say.

- People think I'm successful because I have a professional career with a good income. However, I feel like a complete failure because I abandoned everything that makes me smile to have a "secure" life. At forty, I now wish I'd had the courage to be fueled by faith and walk out the simple yet unique vision God trusted me with. It hurts to my core when people applaud my "success" because I don't feel I've pleased the one who matters most—God.

- I carry the guilt of making it out of the projects, high school, and college, and not returning home. Buying a home and making it on my own, I feel guilty that I made it out and my family did not.
- Guilt ends up making me do a lot. It doesn't keep me from others or from responsibilities, it keeps me from me. . . . I don't rest, I don't relax, I don't exercise. I just give more of myself, my time, my work, my capacity to everyone else. I am capable and see more need and more opportunity, so I push harder.
- I've been on disability a few years due to an autoimmune condition that causes severe weakness. At times my husband has had to carry me upstairs and assist me with daily activities because the weakness was so debilitating. My husband is younger than I am, so at times I live with the guilt of being a burden to him and our son.
- Until I took your survey, I didn't realize how much guilt I carried on so many topics! Maybe I need to go back and see if this is what's holding me back, and learn to let go.

In fact, the survey showed that we feel guilty about *a lot* of different things, such as:

1. Exercise habits (65 percent of participants)
2. Past choices (64 percent)
3. Eating habits (62 percent)
4. Money habits (59 percent)
5. Spiritual habits (not praying, trusting, studying, or meditating enough) (48 percent)
6. Not practicing more self-care (48 percent)
7. Not being more productive (48 percent)

8. Parenting (42 percent)
9. Not living up to expectations (41 percent)
10. Work (37 percent)

Three Truths of Guilt

There are three basic truths about guilt. If you'll come back to these concepts anytime you begin to feel guilty, you will understand better what is going on emotionally and how you should approach the issue. For now, read these three truths and commit them to memory:

Guilt is a message.
Guilt is a debt.
Guilt is an opportunity.

I'll break down each of these truths in a moment, but first, say them out loud: *Guilt is a message. Guilt is a debt. Guilt is an opportunity.*

1. Guilt Is a Message

Guilt is information. It is your conscience trying to tell you that either:

1. you caused harm or did something wrong, or
2. you are *telling yourself* you caused harm or did something wrong *even though you haven't.*

Your job is to accurately read the message of guilt so you can take the right next step to address it appropriately.

Remember this: if you misread the message of guilt, you will react in ways that are unhealthy and counterproductive.

2. Guilt Is a Debt

Guilt means you owe something. Just as a defendant found guilty deserves a sentence, guilt tells you there is a consequence to your actions or lack of actions. Someone must be compensated. You must give up something—your rights, your freedom, your money, your voice. It might mean you do not deserve the good you might otherwise enjoy if you were not guilty.

Remember this: guilt costs you something, and that cost can drive the decisions you make when you feel guilty.

3. Guilt Is an Opportunity

Most powerfully, guilt is an opportunity to change something or accept something. It is up to you to decide which it will be. Rather than using guilt to beat yourself up and make decisions, intentionally choose your response to it. Be curious about guilt, and use it as a chance to

- clarify your values and expectations;
- forgive or be forgiven;
- set or strengthen your boundaries;
- have meaningful conversations;
- grow spiritually and strengthen your faith; or
- be a more courageous, authentic, better version of yourself.

Seeing guilt as an opportunity can bring you hope. Hope energizes you. It shifts your perspective. It helps you set new goals for what your life could be. It empowers you to see that all things can work together for good, that there is purpose in your pain.

Remember this: you have a choice in how you respond to guilt.

What Is Guilt?

Guilt, in the purest sense, is a feeling that indicates we've done something wrong and have caused harm in some way. The guilty party is the one who is at fault. *Cambridge Dictionary* describes guilt this way:

> A feeling of anxiety or unhappiness that you have done something wrong or immoral.[1]

It's not just an emotional feeling; it's a physical one. You can feel guilt as your heart races, thoughts of consequences fluttering through your mind. You can feel it in your churning stomach, upset with regret about what you did or didn't do. You can feel it in your tight shoulders as you dread that conversation with the person who is laying a guilt trip on you.

Merriam-Webster's Dictionary makes two interesting distinctions about guilt in its definition:

1. The state of one who has committed an offense especially consciously
2. Feelings of deserving blame, especially for imagined offenses or from a sense of inadequacy.[2]

So there is the guilt we experience when we do something wrong or commit "an offense." An offense can be a predetermined, agreed-upon set of rules—whether actual laws or expectations within a family, society, institution, or any other social construct. Then there is the guilt that we feel even when we have not actually committed an offense. This is more subjective and is based on an individual's values, strengths, and expectations.

In essence, *guilt is anything you feel you need to apologize for*, even if it doesn't warrant an apology. This is particularly true of guilt trips. (We'll spend a whole chapter on getting over those in a bit.)

Guilt as a Spiritual Concept

In the Old Testament, the Hebrew word *asam* means "guilt" and also "guilt offering."[3] It points to the idea of guilt not as an act but as a relational concept. Guilt is about the relationship between parties. Whereas individual sin is seen as an act of personal failure, guilt is the indebtedness that results from the breach in relationship that such acts cause. Since my sin against you caused harm, there is a breach in the relationship, and I am indebted until I repair that breach, if repair is possible. The focus of guilt from this perspective is on the idea of indebtedness: when you do wrong, you must pay for that wrongdoing. *Asam*—used for both guilt and the offering to absolve it—reflects this concept. If you are guilty, you owe.

> Guilt is *anything you feel you need to apologize for*, even if it doesn't warrant an apology.

But according to biblical scholars, the word *asam* does not appear in the New Testament at all.[4] Nor is there an equivalent word found in the New Testament. The ideas of restitution and indebtedness do not go away. Instead, if someone has sinned against us—or caused harm—we are to let it go. Forgive. And likewise, when we are guilty, God forgives us. In some versions of the Lord's Prayer, "sins" are instead "debts" as we pray, "Forgive us our debts, as we also have forgiven our debtors" (Matthew 6:12 NIV). As a young child, I remember learning the prayer and praying the line, "Forgive us our trespasses as we forgive those who trespass against us"[5] and asking my grandmother what that big word *trespass* meant. It sure sounded important. I didn't realize at such a young age just how profound those words were and how they made my faith different from so many others. Forgiveness is a central theme of Christianity, and the New Testament directly deals with guilt through the once-and-for-all guilt offering of a guiltless Savior. The struggle ever since has been to get the rest of us on board with the idea that we are forgiven—that the lingering feeling of guilt is a self-imposed debt.

What did you learn about guilt in your upbringing? What spiritual messages did you hear, and how have they influenced your feelings of guilt? Your experiences of faith and guilt as a young person can influence how you feel today, for better or worse.

I grew up Catholic. I'll never forget how worried I was when I started going to confession after I was confirmed in the church at eight years old. I was told I would go to confession on a regular basis to tell the priest all the stuff I'd done wrong so that we could say some prayers and then God would forgive me. But that seemed daunting. How on earth was I going to remember everything? Should I keep a running list? What if I forgot something? Granted, the guilt I felt was over third-grade level wrongdoing, like not finishing my homework or sliding a few pieces of steamed okra into my napkin at dinner.

I went to my mom with my concerns. "What happens if I don't tell him everything?" I asked her. "Like what if I just have three sins on my list, but I really have five sins? What happens then? Am I going to be in big trouble with God?" My mom didn't have any answers because deep down she didn't really think it made sense that I needed to go to a priest to be forgiven rather than talking to God directly, but she didn't say that at the time. So I dutifully kept track of my sins, hoping to be absolved of my guilt every few weeks.

Depending on the messages you've heard, either while growing up or well into adulthood, the guilt you feel may be more psychological in effect as you carry the weight of indebtedness for not living up to the rules and expectations of your faith.

Guilt Means "You Owe"

One underlying theme consistently predicts our behavior as it relates to guilt: guilt tells us we owe. Guilt is a debt; therefore it compels us to make an offering of some sort. Whether that offering is a simple apology or an obligation to do something we don't really want to do or a willingness to excuse behavior we wouldn't otherwise excuse, the actions we take when we feel guilty are our offering. If the word *offering* doesn't speak to you, then consider some of these other words that convey a similar behavior:

- overcompensating
- obligating yourself in some way
- excusing otherwise inexcusable behavior, attitudes, or relationship dynamics
- "making it up to someone" for the perceived problem you've caused
- accepting unfair treatment as deserved and acceptable
- being overresponsible while allowing others to be underresponsible

When the guilt we feel is false—meaning we didn't actually do something wrong but feel as though we did—we still feel compelled to compensate in some way, and that can show up in our decisions, words, and actions on a daily basis.

"I owe" can also manifest as "I don't deserve," "I don't belong," and "I have not done enough." And because of these refrains, issues such as perfectionism, insecurity, fear, and comparison begin to surface. It's easy not to recognize it at first, but guilt is often the first domino in a multitude of emotionally toxic behaviors. And this is why we each must go on our own journey toward letting go.

On Trial

If you think of guilt in the most traditional sense of the word, you might think of a courtroom where a person stands accused of a crime. Evidence is presented. A defense is made. A judgment is rendered. If found guilty, a sentence will be handed down.

Our culture has varying opinions about the roles women should play, how those roles should be carried out, and for whose benefit. Many of these opinions are steeped in family tradition and religion, some are derived from the women's movement and images portrayed in media, and others play out right in our own neighborhoods, jobs, or places of worship. It is hard not to be affected by the role models and expectations all around us.

As women, we often unconsciously put ourselves on trial. What do we stand accused of? Exaggerated charges of failing to meet self-imposed expectations. And when we are found guilty, we are sentenced to punishment—often self-inflicted, sometimes indefinite.

When Kim started feeling overwhelmed by the amount of work and commitments she'd taken on, she kept her stress to herself out of guilt. These were the charges:

- As a licensed psychologist, she didn't practice what she preached. *Guilty.*
- When her clients came in feeling overwhelmed, they expected someone who was not overwhelmed themselves. So she was a hypocrite. *Guilty.*
- Her job was helping people be happier. She wasn't feeling happy when she should be happy. *Guilty.*

Her sentence?

- Beating herself up.
- Not allowing herself to take breaks until she got through all the commitments she'd taken on.
- Not being able to enjoy other aspects of life until she straightened out her work life.
- Refusing or deflecting all compliments.

When Kari's marriage ended after her husband's addiction consumed his life, including his lucrative job, she put herself on trial. These were the charges:

- Making a poor choice of husband. *Guilty.*
- Failing to find another father for her children. *Guilty.*
- Hurting her children because now they'd grow up without a father due to her poor choice. *Guilty.*

Her sentence?

- Working long hours in a demanding career to make as much money as possible in order to compensate for the damage she'd done.
- Relinquishing her right to be happy. She didn't deserve happiness after the choice she made.
- Remarrying for the children, not for love.

Terrie spent her twenties finishing college and getting her career off the ground. She loved her work and was passionate about it when she met her future husband. One of the things he loved about her was her independence and passion for living with purpose. But even though she didn't verbalize it, Terrie saw marriage and motherhood as confinement. So as soon as they married, she constantly put herself on trial in her head. The charges?

- Not keeping a clean enough house. *Guilty.*
- Desiring to pursue her work goals, not just family goals. *Guilty.*
- Doing anything for herself to rejuvenate and reenergize. *Guilty.*

Her sentence?

- Always working around the house, staying busy cleaning, cooking, and child-rearing, especially when her husband arrived home after work.
- Suppressing her professional aspirations.
- Abandoning self-care altogether, saying it's selfish.

For years, women's roles were clearly and narrowly defined. In the last fifty years especially, those roles have been challenged and changed in multiple ways. As we have stepped into roles that do not fit within traditions of the past, conflicting opinions and messages leave much more room for doubt. Many women can relate to the feeling that they are doing things differently from their mothers or other matriarchs in their families. So even when they have previous generations' full support, the knowledge that their choices are different can create a sense of self-judgment and self-evaluation that leads to guilt: *Maybe I'm doing this wrong. Maybe the way they did it was better or right.*

Consider what Terrie told me about her own mom when she described marriage and motherhood as "confinement."

"My mom would say, 'I don't have friends. I spend my life with my kids.' There were nine of us and I was the youngest," she explained. "To this day, she still says, 'I stayed home with my kids.' She is prideful about it. And it was a subtle admonishment that that's what her daughters were supposed to do too."

Terrie said it almost feels as though she sometimes repeats it in order to feel better about the fact that she gave up so much. "She's in her eighties now and doesn't have many friends. I think she would have liked to pursue some personal interests, but she didn't. I don't want that for myself or my daughters."

Terrie acknowledged that she often puts herself on trial. Perhaps it is the voice of her mother. Perhaps it is the echo of that message in her church. But even when others don't put us on trial, we often put ourselves on trial. And, it seems, men simply don't—or at least not as often as women.

False Guilt Versus Authentic Guilt

The kind of guilt that led me to write this book is not the guilt of actually doing something wrong. What compelled me is the consistent heavy sigh I get when I mention the subject of guilt to women. It is the sigh of what I call "false guilt," the *feeling* of guilt even though you haven't actually done something wrong.

It's not that we don't do things for which we genuinely need to make amends. We do. But the overwhelming amount of mental and emotional energy we spend feeling guilty about our everyday lives—about the real and legitimate choices we make in our families and our careers, about taking time for ourselves, about not living up to some societal standard of feminine perfection, and about the roles we are supposed to play in our relationships—that leads to false guilt. The pressure is real, and so are the draining feelings of guilt.

So when I use the word *guilt* in this book, I am referring, quite simply, to the feeling that you have done something wrong. I use the word *feeling* intentionally because, as we discussed, you can feel guilty without actually being guilty. And quite frankly, you can be guilty without feeling guilty. Feeling guilty without being guilty drives self-sabotaging behaviors, drives dysfunctional relationships, and creates the low-level anxiety that leaves you feeling you ought to know better, do better, and be better. It causes us to beat ourselves up for never quite getting it right, whatever we think "right" is. This feeling of guilt is what I call *false guilt*. So throughout the book, when I talk about guilt, assume that I am talking about false guilt unless I explicitly say authentic guilt.

Authentic guilt is real. It is the guilt we ought to feel when we do something wrong or cause harm. While we will talk about guilt for things we've actually done wrong and what to do in those instances, most of this book is about false guilt. It is about the nagging feeling that you should be doing better somehow. The operative word here is *should*—that berating word that tells us we don't measure up and therefore need to make up for it somehow.

Authentic guilt isn't so much a feeling but a fact. You yelled at your child out of frustration. You forgot to call your sister on her birthday. You messed up a project at work. You might *feel* false guilt about each of these events, but whether or not you are guilty of them isn't up for question. You are. They happened. And the right thing to do is to own up to it and do what you can to make amends and keep it from happening again. But even in these instances where you've done something wrong, moving forward means letting go after you've paid your debt so you can be free.

False guilt, by contrast, shows up in the mundane of everyday life. It's the constant "I'm sorry" even when there's nothing to be sorry for. I recently watched a young woman trying to get down the narrow aisle to her seat on an airplane say "Sorry" to pretty much everyone she passed. Two hundred people on the plane with oversized bags trying to get to their seats, but she was the only one on the plane apologizing. What was she sorry for? Taking up space, I suppose. Subconsciously, when we apologize, we are saying that we're causing a problem or causing harm, so each time you hear yourself saying it, be willing to ask, *What problem did I cause here?* If there is none, perhaps another phrase besides "I'm sorry" is in order.

What False Guilt Looks Like

I mentioned several examples earlier of women whose false guilt led to decisions with major consequences, and in each instance, the refrain of "I owe" was loud and clear, even if they did not consciously declare it. As Nicole went through counseling to recover from the aftermath of a divorce, part of her healing journey was to trace her steps in order to better understand how she ended up in a marriage that failed. She was reluctant at first to admit it, but she'd had reservations about the relationship both before and after her engagement, and she'd chosen to ignore her misgivings and get married anyway. In fact, she'd been engaged twice. The first time was a few years earlier. That time, she paid attention to the warning signs and broke off the engagement. Her boyfriend was so devastated, Nicole says, he refused to accept it, and the breakup dragged on for months as she explained in a multitude of ways that she did not see a future for them. She apologized. She felt horrible. He begged her to reconsider and asked what he could do to change her mind. Rather than set a clear boundary, she acquiesced to his pleas out of guilt rather than confirming what she'd already said. So it took months of emotional, back-and-forth conversations before she finally ended it. And after she did, she felt absolutely horrible. She and her boyfriend had become engaged within months of meeting, and she explained how it progressed too quickly. She felt too young and not ready to be married, but he appeared to genuinely not understand her perspective and seemed deeply wounded by her decision. She'd never intentionally hurt him or anyone like this, but she had to be true to herself.

As if Nicole didn't feel badly enough already, her mother made comments that made her feel even guiltier about it—comments she repeated almost anytime the subject of that broken engagement came up. "Poor guy. You really broke his heart," she'd say almost jokingly, but Nicole knew there was a hint of seriousness in the comments. His heart had been broken, even if it hadn't been her intention.

A few years later, her former fiancé found his way back into her life. By this point, Nicole had begun to doubt her prospects for love, as she was now thirty and none of her relationships had led to marriage. In her mind, she should have been married by now. The operative word here is *should*. She'd begun beating herself up because "the one" had not come along. She'd started to believe comments from acquaintances and family members that she was "too picky" or "more interested in a career" than love. The comments stung. She had high standards, but she felt that was important if she was to consider being with someone for the rest of her life. She loved her career and she was good at it, but not to the detriment of her personal life. The comments had started to get to her, and she'd found herself even repeating them in conversations with friends. "Maybe I am too picky after all. Maybe I'm not being realistic with my expectations. Maybe I need to play down my career. I mean, I don't think I talk about it too much, but maybe I do . . ." The refrain *I am not enough* began to echo in her thoughts.

She still had doubts that her former fiancé was the right one for her, but time can change people, and she hoped both of them had changed in the right ways. *There must be a reason we've crossed paths again after all this time*, she thought. So she decided to give him a second chance. That's where guilt tripped her up.

During the healing process after the divorce, she looked back over the steps that led her to get married. That's when she pinpointed a pivotal decision that was entirely driven by guilt. Still feeling guilty about the breakup years earlier, and sensing her former fiancé was still wounded by it, she basically made a pact with herself.

"We were on a dinner date," Nicole remembered. "It was probably only the third time we'd seen each other since reconnecting. I still felt deeply guilty about the pain I'd caused him when I broke off the engagement back then. All those years later, I was hesitant to go out with him because I felt I could break his heart again. And if I was to be fair, I at least owed it to him not to get his hopes up. We had a conversation over dinner about the relationship and whether to give it another try. I agreed we could date again, but deep down I told myself I wasn't just agreeing to date. I was agreeing to marry him. Since his feelings for me had not changed over the years, I knew that dating would lead to another proposal. So I felt it would be leading him on to agree to date, and then reject the proposal that would eventually come. My guilt left me feeling I owed him a relationship free of the risk of another breakup."

Nicole was stunned by this admission. It was a silent agreement she made with herself when they decided to date again: *You owe him for breaking his heart. You cannot do that again.*

Being even more honest with herself, she admitted she entered into a relationship with someone who reinforced her guilt and used it to manipulate her. The marriage had been emotionally abusive, and even though she didn't see it at the time, it had started that way. She made excuses for him in a way she didn't for other people. She felt sorry for him, in part, because he always made a point of reminding her that her upbringing was easier than his, and this became an excuse for his narcissistic rage, emotional outbursts, and continuous harsh criticisms. And it all began when Nicole bought into the idea that she owed a debt, rather than forgiving herself for getting engaged too quickly and giving herself the grace to be human and learn from her mistakes. Had she done that, she would not have felt she owed anything, let alone agreed to a marriage she didn't feel entirely at peace about.

When "I Owe" Turns into "I Don't Deserve"

Sherri's variation on "I owe" was "I don't deserve." She wouldn't broach the topic of a raise with her boss, even though it had been three years since she'd gotten her last pay raise. She loved her job. The company was small, but the benefits were great, including the flexibility to arrange her schedule the way she wanted. But her responsibilities had significantly increased while her pay was stagnant. She seemed to feel that she owed the company for the opportunities they'd given her. She had flexibility and money in the bank—more than she'd ever had. She had also worked hard gaining the education and skills to get to the point where she could earn more, something she didn't give herself a lot of credit for. She rationalized that she didn't necessarily deserve more money just because she had taken on more responsibilities.

I know that others who contribute the way I do make more, she thought. *Still, I make more than most people in my family, so I think I feel like I'm being greedy to ask for a raise. Besides, my boss is easy to work for. It's a great company.* So Sherri stayed quiet. She settled for less than she deserved.

The internal refrain of "I owe" in response to feelings of guilt can control your behavior and create consequences that leave you in situations that are unhealthy or unbalanced and take years to overcome. Nicole spent years in a marriage that failed. Sherri gave up thousands of dollars in income over the years, money that could have been used for her family, to eliminate debt, build up an emergency fund, or bless others.

"I Should Know Better / Do Better / Be Better" (or "I Don't Measure Up")

Let me take you back to a morning not that long ago, before I decided to stop beating myself up so much and reclaim my joy. Maybe you've had a day like this.

This is how the morning started: I'm in a deep sleep, dreaming about something I won't remember in a few minutes. I must be outside in this dream because I hear a bird softly chirping and a breeze rustling the leaves in a forest. It sounds like the bird has a friend or two. Wait a minute. He's got a whole family. And their chirping is getting louder and . . .

Dog-gone it! It's my alarm.

I'd set it on that gentle forest sound because I hate to wake up in a state of shock, my slumber interrupted by sudden, blaring buzzers or loud music. So nature sounds it is. And this morning the birds have entered my dreams. Well, I'm half awake. Awake enough to know it's time to get up. Awake enough to begrudgingly recall the ambitious morning workout I planned.

But I'm not ready yet. So, still half asleep, I have a conversation in my head.

This is the morning I'm supposed to get up early to work out before anyone else gets up. It's still pitch black outside. I'll get a head start on my day if I just sit up right now and swing my legs over the . . .

I take a deep breath and sigh. It's a sigh of guilt because I know exactly what I am about to do. I pull my hand from under the covers and reach over and feel for my alarm clock. I know I shouldn't, but I hit the snooze button. The negative emotions wash over me like an extra layer of sheets in my otherwise cozy bed.

Just seconds into my day and I am already feeling guilty.

But that's just the beginning. I miss my workout. *Guilt.*

My mother calls. When I answer, she says, "Oh, I thought you'd be working by now." She's right. I thought I would too, but I'm late! *Guilt.*

I notice the date on my phone. Oh no. It is the day after my high school BFF's birthday, and I forgot to call her yesterday. *Guilt.*

Later, while driving, I have a moment at a red light and don't resist the urge to pick up my phone and check my latest social media post. *Guilt.*

I get to work and open an e-mail from my son's teacher. I forgot to sign the field trip form and the trip is today. *Guilt.*

I see news of a similar business to mine launching something new. Rather than being intrigued, I immediately feel like I am not doing enough in my own business. *Guilt.*

You get the picture. These feelings of guilt were so automatic that I wasn't really conscious of them. I just had a continuous feeling of not measuring up and a belief that I could do better if I just got my act together. It was a familiar narrative, a story I often told myself, until I became aware of my thoughts and began to change them. Guilt isn't always about feeling indebted to another person. Often it is about feelings of not measuring up to our own expectations, including the expectations we believe God has of us.

Authentic Guilt Is a Spiritual Guide; False Guilt Is a Spiritual Detour

From a spiritual perspective, false guilt isn't even "your" guilt. It is a weapon the Enemy uses to steal your joy, condemn the very essence of who you are, and even kill your dreams. If that sounds dramatic, it's because it is. The very mission of the Enemy is to kill, steal, and destroy (John 10:10). And that is exactly what the lies of false guilt do. Unlike authentic guilt, false guilt is a feeling, not a fact. It is the condemnation that whispers, "You are not enough. You're not doing enough. You never get it right. You should be ashamed. *You need to pay.*"

But even when you *have* made a mistake or done something wrong, authentic guilt changes nothing until it leads you to act differently. Conviction about your behavior and a sincere decision to change is what God is after. The Enemy knows that if you wallow in guilt, you will waste your precious time. If you believe your guilt makes you unworthy, the Enemy has won. You won't glean wisdom from your experience or turn the pain into purpose. Instead, you'll see guilt as proof that you have no purpose.

The Five Thought Patterns of Guilt

The good news is, cognitive behavioral research shows that if you change your thoughts, you can change your emotions.[6] This is true of guilt as much as any other emotion. So when you become aware that you are inaccurately interpreting your actions as harmful to others, you can reframe your thinking and choose a more accurate view of the situation. By changing your thoughts, you can change how you feel—you can stop feeling guilty and even start feeling joy. We'll talk about exactly how to do that in the coming chapters. For now, I want you to take note of the thoughts that lead to guilt.

To feel guilty, you must have a thought that causes you to feel that way. That thought is an interpretation of events. It is an allegation, an accusation, and, ultimately, the conclusion you draw about the dilemma you face. I have identified some thought patterns that lead to guilt. While you may word your thoughts differently, they likely fall under one of the following five thought patterns:

> By changing your thoughts, you can change how you feel.

Thought Pattern 1: "I did something wrong."

The most basic cause of guilt is feeling badly for wrong-doing. The concept of "wrong" is shaped by your personal values. Values are what you deem important and meaningful. These values are informed by a variety of sources—your upbringing, your faith, and your culture, to name a few. What you see as wrong, someone with different values may not. And what someone else sees as wrong, you may not. On a societal level, the concept of "wrong" is shaped by laws and institutional or organizational norms. Whether or not you personally think something is wrong, you may be deemed guilty because the larger entity has defined right and wrong. Others can declare you did something wrong, but if your values don't align with theirs, you won't feel guilty.

Thought Pattern 2: "I believe I caused harm to someone or something."

Interpreting your behavior as harmful, even if it is not, generates feelings of guilt. This thought pattern is relational. You feel bad not only because you believe you did something wrong but also because what you did caused pain or a problem for someone else. The consequences are felt by others, not just by you.

Thought Pattern 3: "I didn't do enough."

When you think you haven't done enough, you feel guilty. This can apply in situations where you believe you should help someone, such as an ill loved one, a down-on-their-luck coworker, or even your own child. It can also apply to the expectations you set about how hard you should work and the effort you should put into a project or task. These thoughts are driven by your judgment of how much is enough. So while one person may think they've done plenty, someone who has done more can feel they've not done enough.

Thought Pattern 4: "I have more than someone else."

Guilt about good fortune emerges from the thought that others are suffering while you are prospering. The underlying thought is that perhaps you have an unfair advantage or have received blessings you do not deserve, or that others have experienced misfortune they do not deserve. These thoughts can occur even when you have made good choices that led to good fortune while someone else made poor choices that led to misfortune. The awareness that an element of divine favor has played a role in your good fortune can contribute to these thoughts that the way things have worked out is unfair, that you're just lucky, and you're enjoying more than your fair share of blessings while others have less. After all, why have you been blessed while someone else hasn't?

Thought Pattern 5: "I didn't do something, but I wanted to."

You think about doing things that are wrong. You haven't actually done anything, but the fact that you've daydreamed about it or considered it can cause you to feel guilty. Or maybe it wasn't even a conscious act. You had a dream that you wanted something or did something that goes against your values, and when you woke up, you remembered your thoughts. This thought pattern also applies when you wanted to do something good but didn't follow through. You feel guilty because you never got around to carrying out that good intention.

Don't Let Guilt Make Decisions

Here's the first thing I learned about guilt when I decided it was time to let it go: it was often harder to control the feelings of guilt than it was to control what I chose to do because of those feelings. So I realized I needed to learn to separate my feelings from my actions.

As you journey through life, you might not be able to control whether these thought patterns show up on any given day. Sometimes a thought just comes out of nowhere and tags along for the ride. But it is your decision whether you allow it to get in the driver's seat and start controlling your choices.

By becoming aware of its presence, you can intentionally disarm guilt. Don't ignore guilty feelings. Instead, talk to them—boldly: *I see you there, but I choose not to listen to you. You don't get to make any choices for me. I will actively work to get rid of you, but even if I don't, know that you do not get to make decisions for me.*

Label Your Guilt

Naming or "labeling" your emotions can be an extremely important step to taking control of them, according to researchers.[7] Labeling an emotion when it rises within you creates distance between the emotion and your response to it in a matter of seconds.[8] This is especially important when dealing with a negative emotion such as guilt, because of the tendency to want to react based on the emotion.

Imagine for a moment a decision you've made out of guilt.

Now, imagine if you had simply stopped for five seconds before making that decision, said "That's guilt," and then followed your acknowledgment with a conscious pause and a deep breath.

UCLA researcher Matthew Leiberman calls this "affect labeling."[9] *Affect* is a psychological term for emotional state. He conducted fMRI brain research that showed that when individuals label an emotion, there is a decrease in activity in the brain's emotion centers, including the amygdala. Your amygdala processes play a major role in regulating your emotions and behavior. The amygdala is best known for its role in "fight-or-flight" reactions. When you sense fear, the amygdala processes it and helps you move into survival mode. Feelings of guilt are often accompanied by fear—fear of negative consequences, such as rejection, blame, and disapproval, to name a few. Labeling guilt, and then pausing to notice it and take a deep breath, can give you an opportunity to slow down and process it differently, thereby interrupting the automatic fight-or-flight response.

By labeling your emotion, you raise your awareness of its presence and the danger of allowing it to take over your reactions. Labeling it creates an interruption, which is an opportunity to stop and regain control of your thinking in the present moment. In other words, say to yourself, *Guilt just showed up and is trying to take charge. Stop and breathe.*

I think about that morning with my son Alex after he asked, "Can I eat my cereal at the table?" Imagine if, in the few seconds between hearing the question and responding, I'd noticed my thoughts and said, "That's guilt," and then taken a deep breath so I could respond rather than simply react. Reactions are automatic and often driven by emotion and impulse. Responses are conscious and intentional.

This simple step of labeling matters in the little things we feel guilty about and is particularly powerful in the big things. Imagine if Nicole had labeled her false guilt about breaking up with her former fiancé and paused to take control of her decision to commit to a marriage she was not at peace about. Imagine if Sherri had labeled her false guilt about asking for a raise and refused to let it keep her from speaking up. Most importantly, imagine if you labeled your false guilt the next time it rises up in a conversation, and then paused before reacting. What would you do differently?

Take a moment now to identify the ways guilt shows up regularly in your life. This is the start of your *guilt list*. It's an opportunity to get clear about the guilt you'd most like to conquer in your life—what you want to let go of, even if right now you are not quite sure how.

What to Do Next

WRITE YOUR GUILT LIST

As you sit down to write your list, ask yourself what guilt led you to this book at this time. Remember: the purpose of your guilt list is not to solve anything right now. Simply identify the most critical things that are making you feel guilty. Let's call the items on this list your *guilt triggers*.

I know, I know. You might have a hundred things you could write down right now. You're not alone in that. But for now, I'm inviting you to pick just three. What causes the most pain and anxiety? What's stealing the most peace and joy? That's where

I want you to start. As we continue along this journey, you will be equipped with the knowledge and tools to work through your guilt list and find the freedom you long for.

My Guilt List

1. _____

2. _____

3. _____

Peel Back the Layers

Recognizing and Rewriting Your Internal Narrative

- What's the narrative you've created about your guilt dilemma?
- How do you use the PEEL process to let go of false guilt?
- How do you use the six A's to move through authentic guilt?

To hear Monica speak, you'd think her first child was on a troubled path. But her oldest daughter, Jana, was a twenty-year-old college student with a part-time job who lived at home, was respectful, and was a good big sister to her preteen sister. "I feel like I failed her," Monica said with a mix of regret, shame, and guilt in her voice. "I don't think I was as good of a mom as I could have been to my daughter. Now that I have a second child and I see how much better a parent I am the second time around, with a husband and more resources. I just feel like I didn't do right by her."

This was Monica's most deep-seated guilt. It crossed her

mind daily as she interacted with her daughters. "I can be doing homework with my younger daughter, Gabrielle, and the thought will come to me that I should have spent more time doing homework with Jana when she was younger," Monica said. "It's a terrible feeling, because I am doing the right thing with Gabrielle while judging myself for not doing as much for Jana when she was her age."

I had a coaching session with Monica to help her let go of the guilt that had weighed her down for years. I could see multiple thought patterns of guilt in my conversation with her, and my goal was to help her recognize the patterns and break them. That's where her breakthrough could happen. It's also where your breakthrough can happen.

Coaching as a Tool to Let Go of Your Guilt

Coaching is a powerful, deliberate process that empowers a person to move from where they are to where they want to be. I did one-on-one coaching with Monica, but in this chapter I will teach you the skills to coach yourself. However coaching happens, it can help you pause and notice the many layers of thoughts that create guilt. By peeling back those layers one at a time, you can choose which thoughts to keep and which ones to let go of. And as you let go of the layers that are untrue and even dysfunctional, the weight of guilt will begin to lift from your shoulders, and the lightness of peace and joy can take its place.

I have developed a coaching process specifically to address guilt. I call this process PEEL, an acronym for the steps you will learn in a moment. I have used PEEL with clients and even coached myself using this method. PEEL is rooted in the long-standing research I mentioned earlier around the connection between your thoughts, feelings, and actions.

There are three basic elements to coaching yourself successfully. They are simple, but you must be intentional about them. First, you must pause long enough to quiet yourself so you can notice your thoughts. Second, you must ask powerful questions that get to the truth of the guilt you are feeling. Third, you must be honest in your answers. Depending on the guilt dilemma you face, fear can cause you to avoid, deny, or bend the truth. Don't do it. "Guilt is banished through love and truth," Proverbs 16:6 promised (THE MESSAGE). Refuse to allow fear to keep you stuck, and embrace love and truth instead.

Before we dive into my coaching conversation with Monica, let's take a look at the process of peeling back the layers to find the source of your false guilt.

The PEEL Process

In each step of the process, coach yourself with a powerful question, and keep asking questions until you get to a succinct answer that resonates as truthful.

PINPOINT Your Guilt Trigger

Ask: *What is my guilt trigger?*

Your guilt trigger is the scenario that causes you to feel guilty, whether the guilt is warranted or not. By pinpointing it, you label the guilt, which prompts you to pause. It also raises your awareness that this particular scenario or situation has the potential to cause you to make self-sabotaging decisions. So when the trigger arises, you can be prepared with the knowledge that you need to slow down and use the tool of self-coaching to take control of your reaction before guilt does.

EXAMINE Your Thoughts

Ask: *What am I saying to myself about this guilt trigger?*

This step shines a light on your no-holds-barred thoughts. What do you say to yourself whenever you think of this trigger? Whatever you say to yourself creates your narrative—the story you tell yourself about the situation. But first you must identify what the narrative is. That's what this step does.

We all have narratives running through our minds constantly. Some narratives are helpful and freeing; for example: *I did my best with what I knew and had at the time. I have learned a lot since then, so I am a better person. I forgive myself for what I didn't know, and I am excited about the opportunity to make wiser choices today.* Some narratives are hurtful and guilt-inducing: *I should have known better and done better. It's not fair that my younger child receives better parenting than my older child did. I cheated her!* When you acknowledge your true thoughts about the guilt trigger, you can examine those thoughts and decide whether they are accurate, true, and helpful. A narrative of lies must be rewritten.

EXCHANGE the Lie for the Truth

For each inaccurate thought, ask: *What would be a more accurate thought about the situation?*

This step is your chance to rewrite the narrative so you can begin telling a new and true story about the situation. These new thoughts lead to clarity and power in your decisions about what next step to take. Rather than reacting out of guilt, these thoughts lead you to respond from a place of faith, love, and truth.

List Your Evidence

Ask: *What actions, values, or evidence support the truthful thought about this situation?*

This last step is essential if you want to be confident in the truth of your new narrative. When you examine your thoughts, you are looking for evidence that tells you whether they are true and accurate. In this last step, simply make a list of the evidence that the thoughts you exchanged the lies for are accurate and true. *My oldest daughter is kind and good-hearted. She is progressing consistently through college. She is a hard worker who holds a part-time job while going to school. She's an encouraging big sister and loving daughter. Clearly, I have done many things right in raising her.* It may seem repetitive, but there is an important purpose to this. This evidence supports and reinforces your new narrative—a narrative that will take practice and repetition to live by.

This coaching process to peel back the layers of guilt is not always linear. When breakthroughs occur, it is almost always emotional. Whether you experience excitement and awe or tears of release and relief, what is most essential is your honesty. Your willingness to *tell* the truth about your thoughts creates clarity that allows you to finally *see* the truth—whether that truth reveals authentic guilt that needs to be dealt with or false guilt that needs to be released.

Your narrative is the story you tell yourself about the events of your life. It is the stream of thoughts you choose that explains what and how and why your life has unfolded the way it has. Your narrative influences how you feel and, therefore, the decisions you make about what comes next in your story. So if your narrative says you are guilty when you are not, what comes next may be punishment, compensation, or even shame.

If your narrative says you are guilty when you are not, what comes next may be punishment, compensation, or even shame.

The good news is that you can change the narrative. You can choose new thoughts that create a truthful and freeing narrative. I created the PEEL process as a tool you can use over and over again when you feel stuck in guilt, especially false guilt, and get to the heart of your thoughts. Thought awareness is a resilience skill that can empower you to understand your reactions to certain triggers in your life.

Monica's PEEL Coaching Session

Monica and I did a coaching session specifically to help her peel back the layers of thoughts and guilty emotions that have plagued her. You'll see that as I asked questions, she was able to find the truth and release guilt that had burdened her for two decades. By seeing those layers, she was able to see clearly how her interpretation of her situation created false guilt that she could let go of. It also freed her to acknowledge the authentic guilt she felt and forgive her younger self so that she could be free to truly own every aspect of her story with confidence and without shame or embarrassment. In essence, stopping to peel back the many layers of her story and question the narrative she had created allowed her to take control of that narrative and rewrite it.

Monica's trigger began when she was a teenager. She was a seventeen-year-old high school senior, an honors student who worked hard and loved school, when she became pregnant. The father was her boss at her part-time job. He was eight years older and unwilling to take responsibility. No matter how many times Monica tried to get him to have a relationship with their child over the first few years of Jana's young life, he refused. Determined to make the best of a bad situation, Monica decided to go to college while working full time and raising her daughter on her own. It was hard. Very hard. But she wanted to make the best life possible for her little girl, and she believed furthering her education would enable her to do that.

But trying to do it all took a toll. She had help from family, who looked after Jana while she was working and going to school. But Monica worked until 5:00 p.m. and then headed straight to evening classes, getting home around 10:00 p.m. three nights a week. On weeknights and weekends "off," Monica focused on cleaning and grocery shopping instead of being fully present with her daughter or intentionally teaching her and helping her grow. She beat herself up constantly for this, blaming herself that her daughter didn't yet know what career path she wanted to take, spent her money on movies and eating out rather than saving, and didn't earn grades as high as Monica expected.

I don't know about you, but as I listened to Monica's concerns about her daughter, I thought two things: First, Jana sounded like a normal twenty-year-old. Second, I wouldn't necessarily trace the cause of Monica's concerns about her oldest daughter to her mother's parenting. Believing "I've failed as a parent" because a kid doesn't know what they want to do yet, spends too much of their money on entertainment and eating out, and doesn't get straight As means that even the most loving, consistent, amazing parents could be failures!

When I asked Monica, "What do you feel guilty about?" she answered, "I feel guilty that my daughter is not on the right path, and it is because I should have done a better job as a parent." This is the first step in the PEEL process, to pinpoint your guilt trigger. In everyday conversation, it is easy to simply accept a response such as Monica's as truth and think, *Wow, that must feel awful. I can only imagine the guilt you feel.*

That's why the second step in the PEEL process—examine your thoughts—is key. You cannot accept thoughts as truth just because you have them. And because your thoughts dictate your feelings of guilt, your thoughts deserve attention and curiosity. Start pushing back on them.

Be Curious About Your Thoughts

Curiosity is a tool and a gift. It is your inner detective, eyebrows raised and magnifying glass in hand, asking, "What is that? Is it true? Why? But what about this evidence over here?" Be curious about your thoughts and the causes you assign to the situations that create guilt for you.

> You cannot accept thoughts as truth just because you have them.

For example, when I became curious about Monica's thoughts and subsequent guilt about her situation, I pointed out three things that occurred in succession. It is easy not to notice how they are intertwined in the moment, but they are important to understand:

Trigger $\longrightarrow$ Thoughts $\longrightarrow$ Reactions

This thought-awareness model holds true for any emotion we feel. This powerful tool helps you see how the reactions you have (feeling guilty, then acting out of guilt) are tied to the thoughts you choose when faced with a trigger. When we make it more specific to guilt, this is how it looks:

(Guilt) Trigger (The situation that
causes you to feel guilty)
$\downarrow$
(Guilt) Thoughts (What you say to yourself about
the guilt trigger, which typically manifests as
one of the five thought patterns of guilt)
$\downarrow$
(Guilt) Reactions (Emotion of guilt and the subsequent
actions you take to ease the discomfort it causes)

This simple model can help you become more aware of your thoughts and how they create your emotions and actions. Most people never pause to think about what they are thinking about. When you do, it presents a powerful opportunity to decide if your thoughts are helpful or hurtful.

Let's look at Monica's trigger, thoughts, and reactions.

GUILT TRIGGER	Monica's daughter Jana is not living up to her expectations.

GUILT THOUGHTS	*My early life choices harmed my daughter and have caused her to make poor choices.* *I failed my daughter because I was not there for her the way I could have been if I had not given birth to her at eighteen, if her biological father had been a part of her life, and if she had not spent the first seven years of her life in a single-parent household with a mom who worked and went to college at night.* *Gabrielle has a better life than Jana did because of me, so I have been unfair to Jana.*

GUILT REACTIONS	Monica beats herself up. She feels guilty that her first child wasn't raised with the same benefits as her second child—more of Jana's time, intentional involvement with school, a loving father in the home, and parents who are happily married. Monica is afraid Jana will suffer and that she will repeat the mistakes Monica made. She overcompensates by worrying incessantly about whether Jana will be successful, overlooking Jana's positive choices, and trying to make up for lost time by pushing Jana to live up to higher expectations.

Notice that four of the five thought patterns of guilt show up in Monica's thoughts: *I did something wrong. I caused harm. I didn't do enough. I have more than someone else* (in this case, *My younger daughter has more than my older daughter*).

To take control of anything, you must assess what there is to take control of. That is exactly what thought awareness is— noticing what is there and being curious about it so that you can decide whether the thoughts are healthy and helpful, or unhealthy and harmful. In psychology, cognitive behavioral therapy "helps you become aware of inaccurate or negative thinking so you can view challenging situations more clearly and respond to them in a more effective way."[1] So the tool of Trigger/Thoughts/Reactions (TTR) builds that awareness by peeling back the layers of what you are saying to yourself in reaction to the situations that trigger guilt for you.

Monica experienced a turning point during our session about her daughter. It was an emotional moment as she was heartbreakingly honest about her guilt and the fears behind it, but it was powerful because it ultimately gave her the answers she needed to find freedom.

MONICA: I have failed as a parent because my child is not thriving.

ME: Is she making progress in school?

MONICA: She's doing okay. She's passing classes—Bs and Cs.

ME: She's just not getting the grades you want?

MONICA: No . . . *(anguished and anxious)* and she doesn't know what she wants to do.

ME: Did you know what you wanted to do in your career when you were twenty?

MONICA: *(slow to answer)* No . . . I didn't.

ME: But Jana should know?

MONICA: No.

ME: I'm curious where your expectations of her come
from.

MONICA: Okay. So I grew up in a very rural area. We
didn't have a lot. And so, all of my life growing up,
I told myself something was going to be different.
I wasn't going to continue this cycle. My mom had
me when she was eighteen too. So when I had her
at eighteen . . . *(sigh)* . . . I was like, *No no no, this
is not going to be a repeat (pause, then quiet sobs).*
I just want her life to be so much better than mine
was because I landed in some really hard places,
even as a teenager. I don't want that for her. I told
Jana, you can have things before you're thirty.
You don't have to be figuring out life at thirty-five
and forty years old. Your life can be established,
but you've got to start now. You can't just live
haphazardly and think, *Oh, everything is going to
be okay.* If you work hard now, it doesn't have to
be so hard later. I don't want you to end up feeling
like you've never done things you wanted to do.

I had her at eighteen, and there were so many
things I had planned out for my life that did not
happen. I don't regret having her at all. I just wish
I could have had her later in life so that I could
have afforded her a better life. I don't want her to
have to go through some of the struggles, and even
abuse, that I experienced.

ME: What element of Jana's life at twenty looks like
your life at twenty?

MONICA: *(long pause)* None of it. *(pause)* I guess

because she's not meeting some of the expectations
I have for her, I feel like she's not on the path to
having a successful life.

ME: Does Jana have a child?

MONICA: No.

ME: Are you concerned she's going to come home
pregnant?

MONICA: No.

ME: Did she grow up with the worries you had?

MONICA: *(quiet chuckle)* No. Not at all.

ME: I want you to close your eyes and imagine for a
moment you don't know Jana. Her life is exactly
as it is now, but she's in another family. She's in
college, she lives at home, and she has a job. But
she doesn't know what she wants to do in her
career yet. What are your perceptions about how
her life will turn out?

MONICA: *(quietly and calmly)* She's going to be alright.

ME: Why?

MONICA: Because she is on an okay track. She's
not doing drugs. She's not wild. *(sniffles)* She's
probably in the same typical situations as many
other twenty-year-olds would be in in terms of
spending their money on movies and eating out
and not being sure what she wants yet.

ME: How do you feel saying that?

MONICA: Better. And not feeling so much blame on
myself for what I was thinking in my head—that I
was a failure. That evidently wasn't even the true
reality.

ME: So if I go back to your original guilt statement, "I have failed as a parent because my child is not thriving," is the statement true?

MONICA: No.

ME: Can you replace that thought with a more accurate thought?

MONICA: Yes. *(pause)* Jana is fine. My expectations may be a little bit high. But I haven't failed her as a parent. And I need to be realistic with my expectations.

ME: So what are two realistic expectations you could adopt?

MONICA: *(long pause and a sigh)* With her schooling, being okay that she is attending and she is doing her best. I have to be okay if Bs and Cs are the best she can do and not be so harsh trying to figure out why she can't get As.

And that she's not going to have her whole life together by twenty-one, knowing her major and her career path.

ME: So your new thought is?

MONICA: I am not failing.

ME: What are you doing?

MONICA: Hmm. *(lightness—aha!)* I am continuing to positively impact my daughter's life. I am embracing her college journey. I am going to sit down and map out a budget with her rather than just fussing about my disapproval.

Monica was able to let go of her guilt and see herself as a parent of an adult child who still needed guidance. She was able to forgive herself for past circumstances she couldn't change. Forgiveness allows you to let go of self-anger and other toxic emotions that can cloud your thinking and make it difficult to move forward in a productive way.

While your guilt triggers might be quite different from Monica's, you can see in this coaching conversation how powerful it is to pinpoint a guilt trigger and then examine the thoughts that lead to feelings of guilt. Monica was able to see that her thoughts did not actually reflect the truth, and she exchanged those lies for true thoughts and backed up the truth with evidence. That's the PEEL process. I want to invite you right now to try it for yourself.

Write Through Your Guilt

As you ponder your own feelings of guilt, writing through the PEEL process can be a powerful way to create your own break-throughs. According to researcher and social psychologist Dr. Laura King, writing is a powerful form of thinking.[2] But unlike just thinking, writing creates a record you can revisit and analyze so you can make connections. Use the PEEL process to ask questions of yourself and write your answers.

PINPOINT your guilt trigger: *What is my guilt trigger?*

_____

_____

_____

_____

_____

EXAMINE your thoughts: *What am I saying to myself about this guilt trigger?*

_____

_____

_____

_____

_____

EXCHANGE the lie for the truth: For each inaccurate thought, ask: *What would be a more accurate thought about the situation?*

_____

_____

_____

_____

LIST your evidence: *What actions, values, or evidence support the truthful thought about this situation?*

_____

_____

_____

_____

_____

Authentic Guilt

But what if your guilt isn't *false* guilt? What if it's a message try-ing desperately to get your attention and show you where your actions are out of alignment with your values?

Not all guilt is false. Sometimes we are simply wrong. The only way to let go of authentic guilt is to have enough humil-ity, courage, and integrity to confront it. We are wired for guilt because it helps us align our values with our actions. (We'll learn more about that in later chapters.) It serves a purpose. The anticipation of guilt can keep us from doing things we'll regret. As we'll explore, guilt is not necessarily a negative emotion. If you have done something sincerely wrong, authentic guilt is the appropriate response. But there is a process for moving through this type of guilt as well.

We often resist authentic guilt out of fear. There are conse-quences to be faced if we admit we are wrong, consequences we'd rather avoid. It is a natural human reaction to avoid pain. But remember, guilt is a message. It is one of the ways God guides us to choose what is right, and that includes genuine repentance when we do something wrong. That conviction you feel to tell the truth, to apologize, and make amends? That's a divine nudge guiding you toward integrity and love. No amount of avoidance will banish guilt. Freedom comes with truth, and we must be willing to accept consequences and trust God with the future that unfolds as a result.

Just as there is a coaching process to letting go of false guilt, there is also a coaching process for dealing with authentic guilt. I like to call it the six A's.

1. ADMIT it: *I did something wrong. I caused harm.*
I own up to it. What do I need to admit?

When you truly are guilty, admit it. Tell the truth. You were wrong. You caused pain or damage. It is a heavy weight to live a lie or fight to be right when you know you are wrong. There is power and healing in acknowledging the truth. This step takes humility. You must acknowledge your imperfection, your faults, and your willingness to be accountable for your actions.

2. ASSESS it: *What harm have I caused? What values, rules, or expectations did I violate?*

Consider what damage you've caused by your actions. This allows you to better understand the significance of your actions and what steps you need to take next.

3. APOLOGIZE: *To whom do I owe an apology? What specifically would a sincere apology sound like?*

A sincere apology is one in which you admit and state what you did wrong, how it impacted the other person, your willingness to pay the debt that is owed, and any change in behavior you will make. It takes ownership—like this: "I'm sorry that I didn't contribute my fair share to this project. I realize this put a lot of extra work on your plate at a time when we were already busy."

4. ATONE for it: *Can I make amends? How? If not, what can I do to stop further harm or damage? What consequence should I pay?*

It's not always possible to undo something you've done wrong, but when it is possible, you should do it. If there is a way to make sure it doesn't happen again, do so. And if there is a consequence you must pay, pay it. When appropriate, ask how you can repay the person.

5. ADJUST your behavior: *What lesson can I learn from this? How will I change my future behavior so this does not happen again?*

A truly repentant person changes their behavior. That is the evidence that your apology is genuine. It requires a heart change to not repeat the same mistake or cause harm to others in the same way again. Learn the lesson and change your behavior.

6. ACCEPT forgiveness: *Will I forgive myself? Will I accept God's forgiveness? Will I ask for forgiveness from the person(s) I've harmed?*

We all do things for which we need forgiveness. If you have genuinely walked through the first five steps, you are ready for this last one. Accepting forgiveness means accepting that you fall short, you mess up, and yet God still loves you unconditionally. There may be consequences to pay, but you are forgiven. Forgive yourself. Receive God's forgiveness. And if you are so blessed as to be forgiven by someone you've harmed, receive such mercy and grace with sincere gratitude.

When False Guilt Meets Authentic Guilt: Finding the Grain of Truth

Overcoming false guilt is about clarifying your values and expectations, giving yourself permission to be imperfect, and refusing to go on every guilt trip to which you are invited. But overcoming authentic guilt is about listening to the message that is being offered to you, taking actions that reflect genuine remorse, paying whatever debt is owed, then forgiving yourself and accepting God's forgiveness.

Here's a perfect example of what I mean: I coached Lillian after she found herself in an argument with her sister, Grace, who hurled accusations at her that Lillian felt were unfair. Her sister claimed that Lillian was self-centered and condescending toward her. Grace said that Lillian hogged conversations at family gatherings by talking about her work and professional success constantly and dismissing what was going on in her sister's life as a stay-at-home mom.

Lillian had recently been promoted, and her new responsibilities were exciting, taking her to locations around the world. In the last year alone, she'd been to Hong Kong, London, and Brazil for work. Before this job, Lillian had traveled only in North America, so she was thrilled about the opportunity to see the world. It was a dream come true. Her career had exceeded her expectations, and the one place she felt she could really talk freely about her newfound experiences was with family—or so she thought.

Grace accused Lillian of looking down on her with disappointment and a judgmental attitude, and she claimed Lillian saw Grace's professional choices as a waste of the education their parents had worked so hard to provide. Lillian had never said such a thing to her sister, or anyone else for that matter, and she was mortified that Grace had not only accused her of being condescending and self-centered, but she had repeated the accusation to multiple family members!

Lillian told me in our coaching session, "She's just jealous because I have a lot of freedom, no kids to take care of, and a job I love. I thought she'd be happy for me. To tell you the truth, I'm hurt that she'd accuse me of looking down on her!"

"Hmm," I said as I pondered the situation. "I could definitely see how you'd be overflowing with excitement and wanting to share it with your family. Now you might feel self-conscious about doing that if you think you'll be accused of being self-centered."

"Exactly!" Lillian chimed in. "I thought I was in a safe place, and I am angry because I feel like she's taken that away because of her own insecurities."

"What do you suspect she's insecure about?" I probed.

"She went to college and even grad school—and she's not using her education," Lillian explained. "I think she sees her old classmates moving ahead in their careers, and time is ticking. And she's afraid that when she's finally ready to enter the job market, she won't be able to—at least not in the type of position she'd dreamed of when she was in school."

"Has she told you this is how she feels?" I asked.

"She has. And I agree with her!" Lillian said emphatically. "She claims now that she wants to stay at home, but I'm not so sure I believe that's the truth in her heart."

"So let's just pause for a moment and consider what you just said," I responded, observing her choice of words. "You used the word *claims* to describe your sister's change of heart."

"Yes," Lillian affirmed. "I think she's just saying she wants to be at home full time, but it's just hard to believe. She was so focused just a few years ago, and then she met Kevin and they got married, and suddenly she wants to be a stay-at-home mom.

She'd never mentioned that before! It's just hard to believe she had such a big change of heart."

"So you're judging whether she believes what she is saying about changing her mind? Is that right?" I asked gently.

Lillian paused, then sighed. "I guess that is a judgment," she said reluctantly and with a chuckle of embarrassment.

"Do you think she's wasting her education?" I asked.

"Well, I wouldn't have thought of it like that, but I think my parents are a little frustrated because they made a lot of sacrifices for us in hopes we'd use our educations in pursuit of what we said were our professional goals," Lillian admitted. "And my parents have expressed in passing that they are disappointed to have invested so much in her degrees when she has now chosen another path. I've probably taken on some of their feelings as my own. I mean, our parents didn't even get to go to college, and here we both have master's degrees. Our success is a big deal for our family."

"Is it possible then that you've expressed some of these frustrations in the way you communicate with Grace, even if you don't explicitly say it?" I asked.

"Yes, that's possible," Lillian relented. "It's probably true, actually, even though it hasn't been intentional."

While others might dismiss criticism outright, those willing to find the grain of truth will stop and ask, *Is there any part of this criticism (even if it was said rudely or comes from someone with whom I disagree) that is valid and worthy of being addressed?*

The same can be said of false guilt. Our feelings of guilt can be false while there is a small grain of truth that offers a message we should heed. Noticing the small grain of truth frees you to reject the pieces of a story that are false, while being honest about elements of that story that are authentic and should be addressed. In Lillian's case, the accusation of talking too much about her work led to false guilt. She talked to other family members, and no one else felt the way Grace did. They confirmed her excitement about her success and good fortune. They were proud of her, and no one felt she talked too much about work. For the time being, she decided to be more discerning about what she shared with her sister, realizing that right now, Grace wasn't the best person to talk to about her career. She wouldn't hide anything from her, but she wouldn't go out of her way to strike up a conversation about her job.

The PEEL process worked well for the false guilt. We can summarize it like this:

- **PINPOINT THE GUILT TRIGGER:** Lillian's sister Grace accused her of talking too much about her work.
- **EXAMINE THE THOUGHTS:** Lillian genuinely did not think she talked too much about her work.
- **EXCHANGE THE LIE FOR THE TRUTH:** False guilt almost caused Lillian to stop talking about work altogether with family, but after talking to other family members about it, she decided that wasn't necessary. "I can talk to family about my excitement around my job, but maybe not to Grace right now since it seems to cause some issues."
- **LIST YOUR EVIDENCE:** The evidence that gave Lillian the confidence to drop the false guilt came from talking to three family members who adamantly disagreed with Grace's assessment.

On the other hand, the grain of truth was that Lillian may have communicated in ways that felt condescending to her sister and that went against her values of kindness, humility, and love. So the guilt for this was authentic, and it would not go away until she took responsibility and changed her behavior. That's exactly what she did. She swallowed her pride, called her sister, and had an honest conversation. She explained that the pain she caused wasn't intentional, but she thought about Grace's accusations and realized that she understood how Grace had come to such a conclusion. Lillian admitted it. She apologized. And she changed her attitude. Rather than judging her sister's change of heart about working during this season of her life, she accepted her choices and chose to believe her words.

Grace opened up about her life choices and explained to Lillian that she didn't expect to have a change of heart about her career, but once she had a child, her perspective changed. She wanted to stay home. And she was at peace with that, even though she realized it meant she'd need to adjust her expectations about her career trajectory in the future.

Lillian worked through her guilt using the six A's process:

- **ADMIT IT:** She admitted to her sister that she, like their parents, was disappointed that Grace had put so much into her education and then seemed to give up her dreams rather quickly. She wondered if Grace was being honest about her desires. She acknowledged that these thoughts affected how she spoke to Grace about certain things, and that it was not right.

- **ASSESS IT:** She told Grace that it must have felt frustrating and irritating when she spoke to her that way; therefore Grace probably felt judged. And while Lillian didn't do it intentionally, it was wrong, and she took responsibility for how that affected Grace.
- **APOLOGIZE:** She said sincerely, "I'm sorry for being condescending. And I am sorry for how that has made you feel. I hope you will forgive me."
- **ATONE FOR IT:** After listening to Grace talk about her change of heart, Lillian decided to share with their parents that she understood where Grace was coming from. Rather than remain quiet or even encourage her parents' disappointment, she would help them see things from a different perspective.
- **ADJUST YOUR BEHAVIOR:** Lillian promised to watch her tone when talking to Grace about work and career, and to be more empathetic and supportive.
- **ACCEPT FORGIVENESS:** Grace was surprised by Lillian's admission. She expected Lillian to continue to deny she'd been condescending. Grace was touched and forgave her sister.

What to Do Next

- Choose the guilt trigger from your guilt list that you most want to resolve right now.
- Use the PEEL process to peel back the layers and determine whether it is authentic guilt or false guilt.

- Move through each step of the process to let go of the guilt.
- Decide when you will repeat this process with the other guilt triggers you face.

Declaration

I read the message guilt sends me,
and I respond with love and truth.

Happiness Is a Risk, Guilt Is Safe

The Surprising Habit That Tempts
You to Choose Guilt over Joy

- Why do we feel guilty when we're not?
- Why does happiness trigger fear?

The idea of false guilt is perplexing. Why would we feel guilty when we haven't actually done anything wrong and we aren't responsible for causing harm? As I started down the path of asking why, one particular answer really intrigued me. Perhaps because, unknown to me at the time, I epitomized it.

As I began writing this book, I had many conversations that deepened my understanding of guilt, and how to let go of it and find your joy. But when I brought up one particular moment to Jill Jones, licensed psychotherapist and coach, she said something that stopped me in my tracks.

"Happiness is a risk," she said matter-of-factly. "Guilt is safe."

I stared back at her in disbelief. Happiness is a risk? I'd never heard that. What did this mean? And could it be true?

I've spent many years of my career talking about how

happiness is a choice. Happiness is the one thing we pursue for its own sake. Never have I consciously thought of it as a risk. Call me naive. To me, happiness is what we all want, even if we don't say so. But when I asked her what she meant by the idea that happiness is a risk, I realized that deep down, I behaved as though it were.

As I pondered her statement, I soon remembered the first time I heard the concept of "foreboding joy," described by author and researcher Dr. Brene Brown.[1] I'd never had a term for this phenomenon until then—the sense that even if you're happy now, there's a chance something bad is just around the corner. But although I'd never had a term to describe it, I certainly had felt it for what seemed like my entire life. I believe it was a pattern that unfolded in my childhood. I'm going to give you a glimpse of a few of the stops on my personal journey in hopes that it might provoke thought and clarity about the fears and motives that might drive your own false guilt.

The Vision

I distinctly remember the fall day that I had an epiphany about my life's vision, just as I was turning into the parking space in front of the second-floor apartment I shared with a roommate. I was twenty years old and just a month into my graduate program in journalism at Florida A&M University. It was as if God gave me a glimpse into my future. *You'll write books,* I sensed in my spirit. There weren't a lot of details about the vision, but purpose drove it.

The second message I sensed was this: *As an author, you can have a career doing work you love and also have the flexibility in your schedule to manage both career and family.* Even at that young age, I was already concerned about how I was going to do both. I didn't know what kind of books I would write yet, but this idea resonated deeply with me—both the book writing and the flexible schedule.

I *love* books. As a child, I had no siblings and I learned to read early, so books were like friends to me. I mark periods of my life by the books I was reading and how they affected my thinking, my faith, and my sense of self. I use books like decorations in my house—on coffee tables, in the kitchen, on end tables, bookshelves, dressers—everywhere. So the idea that I might aim for a career in which I actually created books was a dream bigger than any other I had dreamed.

Just six years later, I published my first book. And within a couple of years of that first book, I launched a full-time career writing and speaking. But it would be more than two decades after that fall day before the entire vision came to pass.

I assumed I'd feel happiness, excitement, and sheer bliss upon making the dream I'd laid out so long ago a reality. The last thing I expected to feel upon achieving a vision I'd held in my heart for twenty years was guilt.

Having It All, Including the *Guilt*

Another fall day, twenty-three years later, I realized the thing twenty-year-old Valorie had set out to do was the thing I now felt guiltiest about. The scene was even dreamier than I would have imagined years earlier—I had a husband I'd grown up with in Colorado, an office a half-mile golf-cart ride from my drive-way, family within minutes from home, and a business that was thriving and making a positive impact on the lives of people all around the world. The road had not been easy, but it had been a steady climb.

On this particular day, my husband and I drove our golf cart to drop off our son at daycare, and then I headed right next door to my office. You heard that right. My office literally overlooked the playground at my son's preschool. At the time, we lived in Peachtree City, Georgia, a city south of Atlanta with nearly one hundred miles of golf-cart paths and more than fifteen thousand golf carts. You could drive anywhere on your golf cart—to school, your favorite restaurant, the grocery store. I had timed it: it was a three-minute ride to the preschool and then another fifteen seconds to park at my office right next door.

But that day after we dropped our son off, I remarked to my husband a sentiment I often had.

"I feel so guilty," I said with a loud sigh.

"Why?" he asked, perplexed.

"I feel bad leaving him at preschool. I know I work only three days a week now, but I feel like it's still too much, like I'm doing something bad by working," I answered. Living in a neighbor-hood where the majority of the moms did not work, I often noticed that my life looked a bit different.

That's when my husband stated the obvious in the form of a question. "Wasn't this *your* vision? To write and speak and run your business, so you would have the flexibility to have a career and a family on your terms?"

He reminded me of my own vision. Until that moment, it had not even crossed my mind that I had finally walked into the vision I had set barely out of my teenage years. The journey had been so long that I'd forgotten the destination! I had been intentional and tenacious and not given up on it, even when I felt like losing hope. It took more than twenty years to unfold, far longer than I would've ever imagined. It was a road paved with disappointment and heartbreak and fear and infertility, and then the pure joy of a second chance and a son we were destined to raise. And then the guilt. The dreaded dropoff. No matter that my son was very happy when he walked into the classroom and saw his friends. They hugged and high-fived. They all yelled his name simultaneously when he would walk in the door: "Alex!"

"He loves it there," my husband said, bewildered by my guilt. "That's where his friends are. He's really social. This is good for him. You're a great mom. You're living exactly the life you're supposed to be living." His words affirmed me like a warm hug, reminding me I am on my path, living my values, following my calling. I wanted those words to be my own. I wanted to stop the second-guessing and just rest.

By inserting negative emotion into situations that would otherwise be joyful, I was, in a way, shielding myself. Life was good, but it was not *too* good. *If something goes wrong,* I seemed to think, *perhaps the fall won't feel quite so devastating because it wasn't perfect anyway. I wasn't really* that *happy.*

Happiness requires courage. It requires effort. It takes tenacity and perseverance. It takes hope. But hopes can be dashed. Disappointment is always a possibility.

I learned this lesson early in connection with the happiest time of my childhood—my summers. I spent my summers with my grandparents in South Carolina, starting at the age of three. My days were carefree, fun, loving, and filled with family. Those summers helped shape who I am, where I come from, and my drive to do something meaningful with my life.

During my seventh summer there, Granddaddy explained he had cancer, a word I don't think I'd ever heard before then. We spent the summer going to doctor's appointments, and Granddaddy made comments about this being our last summer together—comments Grandmama would quickly dismiss. But he knew. Just after Labor Day, he died. All these years later, I cry typing those words. He believed in me big time. He loved me. He made me feel special.

But his death was the beginning of the many ways my world would keep changing just about every two years. I remember crying in Grandmama's lap, unable to fathom that we'd never see him again. She wiped the tears from my face as she promised, "I'll be your grandmama and your granddaddy from now on. It's going to be okay." But she couldn't keep that promise long. Two years after Granddaddy died, Grandmama died too. It seemed as I got used to one unwanted reality, a new one would set in. Then two years after her death, my parents separated and my mother moved ninety miles away to another state. Two years after that, we lost our home. Two years later, my parents finally divorced.

I don't tell you these things to make you feel bad for me. We all have our stories. My point is that I constantly felt like my world would be snatched from beneath me. "Don't get too happy, because this probably won't last long!" was the persistent message I received. I was indeed scared to be happy because I was afraid of losing that happiness.

Happiness, for me, was risky. It meant risking disappointment. Fully embracing happiness meant expecting that happiness would hang around when I didn't really believe it would. The higher my happiness level, the more devastating I feared the fall would be. So if I could just find a way to bring my happiness down a few notches, I could feel a bit safer. I could cushion the inevitable fall I so anxiously yet subconsciously feared.

As a result, I tended to bring some sort of negative emotion into my life to cope. When I finished school and started an amazing life in my early twenties, it was worry. I worried I would be struck with some awful tragedy. I remember sitting in church catastrophizing about all that could go wrong, even though everything seemed to be going right! I would pray that God would let me continue to be happy and blessed, but I was afraid I was asking too much, given that I already had such blessings. When I was engaged to my husband, I worried something would happen before the wedding. It had been such a long road to true love and marriage. Would it really happen? I counted down the days, fearing the rug would be snatched from beneath me before our wedding day, but I was too afraid to tell anyone my anxious, irrational thoughts. Then we married. My dream had unfolded. And while the worry didn't entirely disappear, it mostly went away as my days filled up with new responsibilities as a wife and bonus mom . . . and then mom. But joy did not replace the worry. Instead, I traded worry for guilt.

"It isn't that women are afraid to be happy," Jill Jones, a Georgia-based licensed clinical social worker, elaborates. "They are afraid of *happiness*."[2] It's as though we believe that God will look down and say, "That one right there! She has too much happiness!" To make matters worse, she points out, many people believe two things from a religious perspective: (1) that you must earn your way into heaven by always doing what is right, and (2) that it is our job as humans to suffer a bit. So we use guilt and fear to manufacture a little bit of pain to put alongside our happiness to avoid angering God. As Jones puts it, "We think, 'This isn't fair. What did I do to deserve all of this?'"[3]

Let's take a closer look at the issues at play here:

- Our desire to be happy
- Our fear of happiness
- The safety of unhappiness
- The benefits of guilt

Our Desire to Be Happy

When I wrote *Happy Women Live Better*, I talked about happiness as the motivation for every goal we set. Basically, happiness is the one thing we pursue for its own sake. Everything else, we typically pursue because we believe it will ultimately make us happier if we attain it. Whether it's a relationship or a career opportunity, money or a weight-loss goal—or even having more faith—we pursue goals because ultimately we think we'll be better off—*happier*—when we reach the goal. No one asks you *why* you want to be happy. It's a given. Not even the most pessimistic, unmotivated grouch sets a goal to have their most miserable, unhappy year ever.

So what is happiness? It is subjective well-being. I can't tell you you're happy or not happy. You are the judge of that.

The problem is, the road to any goal is a winding one. Obstacles and challenges abound. There is often a price to pay in exchange for reaching the goal—and we pay it in time, energy, and sacrifice.

Generally, we want to feel good and be happy. It's a basic human instinct. But happiness is a journey paved with choices. In fact, research shows that while about 50 percent of happiness can be attributed to the temperament with which we were born, 40 percent of happiness lies in the intentional choices we make.[4] The fact that we can influence our own happiness through our choices is powerful. But when the choices that could lead to more happiness get tangled up in our false guilt, it complicates matters.

Additionally, when our beliefs around happiness—religious or otherwise—cause us to feel that the desire to be happy is somehow selfish, unfair, or unspiritual, guilt will drown it out.

Fear of Happiness

Risk is the reason most people never step out in faith for their big dreams. Whether it's the risk of failure, the risk of rejection, or the risk of uncertainty, the unknown ignites fear. The what-if question arises—and for most people, that means stop. *What if I fail? What if I'm wrong? What if they don't like my decision? What if _____?* If you're human, you've likely asked what-if questions that left you paralyzed with fear.

No matter the goal, many of us tend to overestimate the risk of pursuing something that could make us truly happy. It's a protective mechanism. Better to overestimate the risk of happiness and avoid pain than underestimate the risk and find yourself living in regret for your choices. Fear

> No matter the goal, many of us tend to overestimate the risk of pursuing something that could make us truly happy.

is powerful; our brains are wired to pay attention to it. But we can treat unfounded fears as seriously as well-founded ones. So when those what-if questions kick in and our fears go into high gear, our brains naturally want to avoid the potential danger (code: pain) that fear tells us could be on the horizon.

If happiness is a risk, it also comes with its own set of what-if questions:

- What if I don't deserve happiness?
- What if I'm happy while others are suffering?
- What if I can't maintain this level of happiness or success?
- What if others become jealous?
- What if my naysayers are right and end up saying "I told you so"?
- What if my happiness disrupts my relationships?
- What if finding happiness takes longer than I expected?
- What if what I think will make me happy doesn't?
- What if _____?

These aren't typically questions we ask aloud. Sometimes they're refrains that play quietly and persistently in our minds. Sometimes they're so much a part of our mental landscape, it doesn't occur to us that they are making us fearful.

To be happy, you'll have to give up the certainty of what you know. Subconsciously, for some, it feels safer to hold on to what you know than to venture out of your comfort zone. But if you make the changes in your life that you're afraid to make, you just might succeed at becoming happier than you've ever been.

The Safety of Unhappiness

If happiness is a risk, then unhappiness is safe. It's certain. You know what to expect. Guilt is one of many negative emotions that create unhappiness. When you feel guilty, you take action out of that guilt, and those actions become your norm. You expect it, and so does everyone else. It's bondage, but you know what the boundaries are—the boundaries that keep you confined to a life that is not authentic, although it certainly is familiar.

The safety of unhappiness is the security of a comfort zone. But is isn't actually safety—it's the *feeling* of safety. You might not like being unhappy, but at least you know what's coming. You know what arguments to expect, whom to appease, and how you will feel.

To be happy, you may have to set boundaries. You may have to stop taking responsibility for things that are not your responsibility and allow others to step in. You may have to own your values and opinions, which could be different from the values and opinions of those around you. You may have to stop pretending things are okay that aren't. You may have to stop blaming others for problems and take ownership of your role, even if it is a role for which you feel guilty. And you may have to do the hard work of evaluating, learning, and forgiving yourself for past choices. None of these actions are in most people's comfort zones. They feel risky. But to be happy, these are the types of actions you'll need to take.

Ridiculous as it may sound, we can become so comfortable with the absence of happiness that when there is no reason to be unhappy, we manufacture one. Worry. Discontentment. Envy. Blame. Drama. And, yes, guilt. So when I say guilt is safe, what I am saying is that guilt moves your emotions from positive to negative—to a place that may feel more familiar, more comfortable. It is up to you to decide when you are ready to release the false guilt and reclaim your joy.

The Benefits of Guilt

When you feel false guilt, you receive a benefit of some sort, even if you cannot easily articulate it. Remember I said that we can choose from a variety of negative emotions to create unhappiness because it feels safe? Well, guilt is a negative emotion with benefits many of the others don't have. For one, guilt makes you look good. After all, if you feel guilty, it means you're concerned. You care. You want to do the right thing. If others sympathize with you, even better. But even if not, for the sake of others' perceptions and reactions to you, guilt can also help you feel better about a situation. I'll show you what I mean in a moment as I give you a tool to deal with this.

Use Self-Coaching to Dive Deeper

Guilt is a negative emotion with benefits many of the others don't have. For one, guilt makes you look good.

One of my favorite tools is to combine coaching with writing to peel back the layers of a dilemma in order to better understand what's really going on. While it's great to have a coach to walk you through your challenges, it's even better to possess the tool of self-coaching so that you can use it whenever and wherever you need it—not just in a coaching session. The process is simple, but again, here is what to do:

- Pause. Get quiet.
- Pray for wisdom and the courage to be completely honest with your answers.
- Ask a powerful question that helps you get to the root of whatever fear or obstacle holds you back from what you want in your situation. For example, *What am I getting out of feeling guilty in this situation?* Write or dictate your answer.
- Follow up with the next question that helps you peel back another layer. For example, looking at your answer to the previous question, you could follow up with, *What does this give me?* or *In what way does this feel safe?* Write or dictate your answer.
- With only the powerful questions that peel back these two layers, you can begin to see how guilt creeps into your thought process and creates a story.
- Then take a look at what you actually want instead of the guilt—joy. Ask this question: *What would it look like to feel joyful in this situation?* If it isn't a situation in which joy is an appropriate emotion, then perhaps instead use the word *peaceful.* Write or dictate your answer.
- Finally, in light of the honest answers you have given here, ask: *What is the wise thing to do?*

Self-coaching isn't an exact science, but it works. Take the time to slow down, notice the guilt you're feeling, explore it, and make intentional choices about how you want to move forward.

To help you see how this works, I'm going to share how I used this process in relation to my writing. I often feel laden with guilt when I don't write as much as I was planning to, or, worse yet, have a looming deadline. But because I actually love writing, my guilt doesn't really make sense. These two opposing facts drain my happiness. I have allowed this to happen many times in my career. I wondered if this idea that "happiness is a risk and guilt is safe" applied. And as I self-coached, I discovered that, in fact, guilt made me feel safe.

Here's a peek into my self-coaching journal. Notice how I acknowledged whatever came to me and then asked additional questions to peel back more layers:

What do I get out of feeling guilty when I don't write? What's the benefit?

I get to somehow feel like I'm really trying.

I get to feel like I'm struggling.

I get to feel sorry for myself.

I get to convince others to feel sorry for me.

I get to keep procrastinating.

What do all of these things give me?

These benefits give me an excuse to keep doing what I am doing. This allows me to feel like writing somehow has to be hard as opposed to being something easy.

What does feeling like writing has to be hard give me?

Less happiness, which is punishment for not writing since writing is what I should be doing. To not write and be happy is not allowed.

What would it feel like if writing was joyful?

It always feels purposeful, and I always feel deeply satisfied when I write. But I also wonder if I can keep it up. There is the pressure of success that second-guesses whether I will keep succeeding. It's like impostor syndrome. Was it a fluke that I already wrote twelve books? Did I just luck out or can I do this again? Can I write number thirteen?

When I wrote my first book, it was dreamy.

But wait. This isn't true! My first book was my third attempt at writing a book. And I finally got going when I got sick of hearing myself talk about writing a book but not actually doing it! So what am I talking about, it was "dreamy"? Maybe once I got down to business it was dreamy, but before that, it was the same paradigm—not writing, then feeling guilty for not writing. A license for self-pity and excuses.

This is my default. This is "safe."

But what if, in this book process, I actually make writing joyful? What if that becomes a part of my book journey?

What if rather than feeling guilty, I feel happy? What would it take to feel happy instead of guilty during the writing journey?

I would have to let go of excuses. I'd have to accept that finding time is challenging and then find a way to write in spite of the challenge.

Getting out of guilt requires discipline. And basically what I'm saying is I have to choose discipline over guilt if I want to be happy. I have to just do it if I want to be happy.

Why else should I not feel guilty? Let me rephrase that: Why else could I feel happy writing my book?

Because God gave me the gift and a mission around writing! Because writing is the most central and purposeful element of my work, and everything else flows from it! Because I want to be happy! I want to be happy! When I remember that, then I behave as though it is true. I don't want to wrestle with guilt. I want to be happy.

The key here is remembering. My safety net is a default rooted in fear.

So what about you? How might this idea that "happiness is a risk and guilt is safe" apply to a situation on your guilt list? You might resist this idea a little bit, but I invite you to consider it as a possibility. When we hold on to something (guilt) for a long time, even though we claim not to want it, it is important to be curious about our reasons for not making a change. Our reasons for staying stuck are often not obvious—or logical—but when we become clear about the things that cause us to stay right where we are, mired in guilt, then we can make new choices that free us to conquer our fears so we can embrace joy wholeheartedly.

What to Do Next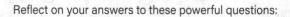

Reflect on your answers to these powerful questions:

- Are there things you have or have not done that leave you feeling you don't deserve deep happiness? What are those things? Rather than accept the idea that you somehow don't deserve happiness, consciously choose happiness. Choose joy in spite of your shortcomings. You are the only one who can make this decision, and you'll have to be intentional about it. When we develop thought patterns of guilt over a long period of time, they can become our default until we practice new thought patterns intentionally and persistently.

- Do you feel as though you still need to pay for past mistakes, choices, or missteps before enjoying complete peace and joy? If so, haven't you paid long enough?

- Our behaviors are motivated by avoiding pain or embracing joy. What are you getting out of holding on to guilt? Rather than insist the answer to this is "nothing," sit with this question quietly. Be honest, and prayerfully reflect on the answer.

- If you let go of guilt, how would that change the dynamics in your relationships? Imagine what freedom would look like in your relationships. Imagine what joy and peace could emerge.

The Guilt Gender Gap

Why Research Shows Women Are Guilt Prone

- Why do women feel guiltier than men?
- Do women today experience more guilt than previous generations did?
- Why does it matter whether women feel guiltier?

There is a long list of reasons women feel more guilty than men, not the least of which are the relentless expectations that tell us who we should be and how we should be. Plus, research shows women have higher emotional highs and lower emotional lows, which means we notice and feel emotions more readily.[1] Add to that the fact that perfectionism is largely a women's issue and that we women can be hard on one another—especially on our daughters—and you have a recipe for dousing your joy with guilt.

Jessica's husband worked on movie sets in California, and she managed accounts for her employer around southern California. While she occasionally needed to take short trips for work, her husband left for up to eight months at a time to shoot movies.

"I don't think my husband ever felt guilty," she said. "He never felt like a bad dad for traveling. Instead, he genuinely felt his job was a great opportunity for our family."

Not only did he feel good, but others' reactions to him were different. "When I was traveling," Jessica said, "people asked all the time, 'How can you be away from your child? This must be so hard for you.' I would be gone for a few days. My husband was gone for months at a time, and no one ever asked him how he did it or whether he felt guilty. He felt sad and he missed us, but he never felt guilty."

In a sense, Jessica felt as if she were on trial. Others seemed to question her choices, and she then began questioning her own choices. Her husband felt no such pressure.

Are Women Guilty of Feeling Guiltier Than Men?

According to a study in the *Journal of Personality and Individual Differences*, there is a guilt epidemic among women.[2] The emotion is tied to the habit of self-criticism, according to the study. "Self-criticism," of course, is just another way of saying "beating yourself up." And women are far more likely to do it.

A habitual guilt seems to accompany women. We are simply guilty of being guilty.[3] It is often guilt over little things, a self-criticism based on expectations and ideals that are hard to live up to every single day. Men, on the other hand, tend to feel guilty about "big things" like cheating or making a bad choice with major consequences.

So women feel guilty more often, for more reasons, than men

do. Why do we, as women, seem to struggle with guilt more? Digging into the research led me to some interesting insights and generalizations about why women may be particularly prone to guilt.

Women are more "other-focused."

Psychologists point out that (most) guilt requires us to think about others, making it an "other-focused emotion." This is unlike "ego-focused emotions," such as happiness or pride. Those who view themselves as closely connected with others have predominant emotions that are other-focused. This is a trait that is more prominent in women than men.[4]

> Women feel guilty more often, for more reasons, than men do.

Women have a more complex range of emotions.

Perhaps this doesn't come as a surprise, but research backs it up. Gender differences in emotions are evident in children as young as three years old. Women experience higher highs and lower lows than men do.[5] So when we feel happy, the emotion is more intense. But when we feel negative emotions, such as guilt, those emotions are also more intense.

Women tend to be more empathetic.

Research shows that women are more sensitive to and skilled at reading others' emotions. In studies, when given hypothetical situations, women show more complex knowledge and nuance of emotions in others than men do. This heightened awareness can make us more sensitive to the impact of our actions on others.[6] Thus guilt can ensue more readily.

Men may be guilt deficient.

A study by a group of psychologists in Spain suggests that men are "guilt deficient." Or maybe a more generous phrase would be to say they lack "interpersonal sensitivity." This simply means they are much less likely to feel interpersonal guilt—guilt about how their actions, or lack thereof, impact others. This is aligned with the finding that men are less empathetic than women. Guilt generally requires empathy. Empathy in men tends to increase later in life, beginning in their fifties.[7]

Women are more prone to perfectionism.

Perfectionism is largely a women's issue, according to research.[8] And it is rooted in expectations and standards that often cannot be met. So where does the guilt come in? If you believe you *should* be able to meet standards that are elusive, feelings of guilt can emerge when you don't.

Women's explanatory style is more likely to be self-blaming.

Explanatory style, or "thinking style," is a concept developed by legendary psychologist Dr. Martin Seligman.[9] It describes how people explain the causes of "good" events and "bad" events in their lives. Those who blame bad events on personal traits over external factors can feel less optimistic about their ability to overcome obstacles and succeed in future attempts at the same goal.

Women worry more.

Women and girls of all ages worry more than their male counterparts. Research shows that girls as young as three or four years old worry more than boys, and elderly women worry more than elderly men.[10] And what is worry? It is fear of the future. It is meditating on what might go wrong. It is conjuring up worst-case scenarios and rehearsing them in your head, and stirring up fear from the worst-case outcomes you imagine. Worry is ruminating on the possibility that something might go wrong.

Worry is not guilt, but habitual guilt over everyday matters is a form of worry. It is worrying that you are not doing things right, that you're not doing enough, that you're not good enough, that you haven't done enough. And ultimately, whatever the "enough" is that you have fallen short of, the essence of your worry is that there will be a price to pay—and that price scares you.

Women face increased expectations.

Women today face a ton of expectations that generations past simply did not have. Much of this comes from positive advancements—more educational and professional opportunities, for example. But this also leads to more choices, and therefore, more opportunity to second-guess those choices or feel guilty about making the wrong choice. Some of these high expectations are connected to increased pressure to earn money now that the dual-income household is the norm, even though women are still the primary caretakers of children and the household.

This conflict can create feelings of guilt. For example, studies show women are 30 percent more likely to feel guilty than men when we have to work during personal time—and that guilt applies whether women are married or single, mothers or not. Those who feel most guilty, though, are mothers of young children.[11]

Women are primed for guilt by cultural influences.

Girls and women are encouraged to play nice and to nurture relationships. The fact that these habits are nurtured in girls more than boys can cause women to take on the responsibility of others' feelings. And we are bombarded with images of being the perfect mom, wife, and worker, with the perfect body, home, and hair. These expectations can whisper urgently to us at the most inopportune times, dredge up guilt, and affect our choices in ways that create unnecessary stress.

Just notice next time you're in front of a magazine rack at the store. Sure, men's magazines have cover articles about bettering yourself, but the focus is on bettering yourself for you, not for others. Women's magazines often write from the perspective of being something for other people rather than just being something because it will make you a better *you*. That subtle difference in focus means that if you can't live up to an ideal, you aren't just disappointing yourself, but you are disappointing the world around you and the people closest to you.

Women are not always supported by church culture.

Women of faith are rarely affirmed for their roles in the workplace. We are encouraged as wives and mothers, but rarely as leaders and professionals, employees, coworkers, and bosses. The silence about this facet of our lives is loud. The message that can be inferred is that work and leadership for women is not worth addressing in church, even though more than two-thirds of women spend the biggest chunk of their time in the workplace.

While it might be traditional for women not to work, it is not distinctly biblical. The quintessential example of womanhood, the Proverbs 31 woman, diligently ran her household, honorably supported her husband, and profitably managed her business affairs.

An age-old question asks whether all the differences between men and women are biological or if some are environmental. Do women feel more guilty because we are wired differently? Or does our culture and upbringing play just as important of a role? The answer is both. And each of us is different. Perhaps your guilt is influenced more by innate traits while mine is more influenced by what I learned growing up—or vice versa.

Why Does It Matter That Women Feel Guiltier?

So why does all this matter anyway? For one thing, excessive guilt is a symptom of major depression. Women are twice as likely as men to suffer from depression, and over the last fifty years, the average age of the first onset of depression dramatically dropped. Most women who are depressed today first experienced depression as teenagers. Just a generation ago, the average age at first onset was the late twenties. While excessive guilt does not cause depression, the fact that it is a symptom tells us something very important. It is one of the results of a negative emotional state. When our mental state is negative, we often ruminate on the negative. And negative emotions, while essential in some ways, can take a toll not only on our mental and emotional health but on our physical health as well.

Positive emotions, on the other hand, have been shown to

make you more successful, healthier, and more likely to attract opportunities and relationships that are supportive and purposeful. Feeling good is good, and the habit of feeling bad and feeling guilty can become a norm that is addictive because it feels safe. You can break out of the habit by exchanging thoughts of guilt for permission to be happy and joyful. Guilt does not have to become a way you pay for the debt of good fortune in your life. Let yourself be uncomfortable and even afraid, but still embrace the joy that is in your life. And remind yourself, *feeling good is good.*

Reject the Guilt

When you understand that you might be more susceptible to guilt simply because of your gender, and that the impact of guilt can have significant health consequences, you can treat it as a wake-up call. It's so important to become more aware of the messages that cause you guilt, whatever the source. And you must reject those messages for your own well-being. As I mentioned earlier, as women we often joke about the chronic guilt we feel, as though we should expect it and accept it as a part of life. But why should we, especially when doing so takes an emotional and physical toll?

You can reject that notion. You don't have to be one of the guilt-prone women who carries false guilt alongside her. You can be a woman who unapologetically avoids guilt trips and false guilt. If you choose to do that, you'll be a light to women still bound by the expectations and values that may not be their own.

What to Do Next

Notice your tendency to gravitate toward false guilt or negative emotions and intentionally look for reasons to choose joy. Keep this message in front of you: *Feeling good is good*. Put it on your bathroom mirror or in the closet; even set a reminder in your phone. When false guilt bubbles up, attempting to steal your joy and make you afraid, remember that joy is good and you have permission to embrace joy wholeheartedly without apology and false guilt.

Own Your Values

If You Don't Decide What Matters to You, Others Will Decide for You

- Whose values are you living by?
- Are you willing to own your values?
- What are the expectations you have that are triggering your guilt?

Simply put, values are the things in life we deem important. We can declare our values and rattle off an impressive-sounding list in conversation with others, but the true test of our values is easily revealed in what we choose to *do* every day.

You live your values even if you don't know what your values are. Values are an expression of what you really believe. When you put your phone down to look your loved ones in the eye when you talk to them, it is an expression of your values. It says, "I value my connection with you, and I value what you have to say." When you scroll your social media feed while your loved ones are trying to talk to you, it is also an expression of your values. It says, "What I'm looking at on my phone is more important than you right now. I do not value what you have to say over my impulse to see what my friends on social media are posting today."

Guilt ensues when our values are out of alignment with our actions. When your actions do not line up with what you say is important, you must reckon with the fact that, in that moment, your values are a lie. It is that lie that creates the guilt.

But what if your values aren't even *your* values? What if the values were told to you? What if you've adopted others' values and never stopped to really question whether you agree with them?

Such was the case with Patricia. During the school year, her husband was in charge of getting their two daughters ready in the mornings. He was good at it and enjoyed it, and Patricia got to get a little extra rest before she headed out into her workday. The routine seemed to work well, except when the subject came up in conversation with her mother. The two are very close, and Patricia holds her mother in high esteem, especially in her role as a parent.

"My mom feels that my husband should not get our daughters ready in the morning—that as a mother of daughters, this should be my role and responsibility," she explained. But years of guilt, followed by some deep introspection, led her to a simple but profound aha moment: "Those are my mother's values. *My values* are that we are a married couple who shares the raising of our children."

It took a long time for Patricia to see that her expectations were rooted in values that were not even her own. So although her actions were out of alignment with the values she claimed, those values were someone else's that she chose to adopt.

What Are Your Values?

Your values resonate deeply. You are drawn toward them effort-lessly. They aren't just what you think is good; they are what you celebrate and measure success by. They are what you want to be remembered for, what you will sacrifice and go the extra mile for.

If you could only choose your top three to five values from this list, which ones would make the cut? What matters most to you?

excellence	sincerity
adventure	compassion
community	ministry
freedom	patience
beauty	control
humor	courage
productivity	risk
empowerment	fun
growth	security
creativity	preparation
achievement	strategy
education	wealth
romance	independence
service	charity
partnership	purpose
joy	fairness
sensitivity	righteousness
integrity	holiness
commitment	affection
professionalism	perfection

truth	curiosity
being a role model	communication
change/transformation	love
abundance	family
spontaneity	expression
victory	health
support	fitness
energy	political consciousness

Owning your values means accepting the fact that you might be different from those around you. Truth be told, you might actually discover that you aren't the only one who holds similar values.

Emily loved her work. She had two children, and her strong faith and outgoing personality kept her plugged in to her church community. In her Chicago church, she found herself surrounded by working mothers like her. In fact, it was the norm—and pretty much all of them seemed to feel guilty about being away from their kids all day. They mentioned their angst in passing with comments during book club get-togethers and Bible studies.

But Emily didn't feel guilty. "I'm a much better mom because I work," she said. "I'm a better person all around using my gifts and making a contribution to the world and my family. And I feel my children are well-adjusted and better off having a mom who works. I have no guilt about it whatsoever.

"What I do feel guilty about is the fact that I don't feel guilty. When other moms at church talk about how guilty they feel, I just stay quiet now. I used to pretend I knew what they were feeling, but then I felt guilty because the truth is, that was a lie."

The norm around her was guilt. Guilt became a shared

experience over which to bond, and Emily didn't share it. When Emily made the decision to stop pretending to feel guilty and instead be honest about her feelings, something pretty interesting happened. Other moms perked up. They were curious about how she could feel that way because, quite frankly, they wanted that feeling too. At least one other woman she was connected with admitted to feeling similarly.

"There's basically this culture within the church that says women are supposed to be wives and mothers, but it doesn't really celebrate other facets of who we are," Emily observed. "Even in this day and age, I think women can feel the pressure to conform to ideas that are not necessarily biblical, but cultural. By telling the truth, I was able to open up a discussion among the women in my church group about what it means to be a professional woman of faith."

Which Values Drive Your Guilt?

Your values are underlying beliefs that guide your decisions and actions—and they form the thoughts that lead to those decisions and actions. Your thoughts do not occur in a vacuum. They are based on your experiences, the lessons you've learned, your environment and culture. You can evaluate the origin of a thought by clarifying the value that created it.

This is a critical part of the process of letting go of guilt. Why? Because thoughts—what you say to yourself—lead to reactions. Reactions are what you feel, say, or do—in other words, emotions and actions. When you change what you think, you can change your reactions. You can change the *feeling* of guilt.

Counterproductive thinking leads to the emotion of false guilt, the experience of feeling guilty even when you have not actually done anything wrong. Before you can change your counterproductive thoughts about guilt, it helps to identify the values that birthed those thoughts. This is where many of us get tripped up.

False guilt is not caused by what happens, but by what you say to yourself about what happens. What you say to yourself is driven by the values you embrace. And you have a choice about which values you embrace and which ones you reject. It takes awareness and intention, but the choice is yours—and it unlocks the process of letting go of the guilt.

We must recognize when we are holding on to values rooted in beliefs that are unhealthy, unhelpful, and, in some cases, spiritually misguided. So I want to help you slow down for a moment to clarify the values that lead you to feel guilty and determine whether they are your authentic values. When I say "authentic values," I simply mean this: Are they truths that best reflect the life of joy and freedom you want? When you live by values that are authentic to you, you "own" them. You are unapologetic about them—kind, but firm.

In my own life, I have used this process repeatedly to let go of guilt. It is a process I also use with my clients. I use a combination of techniques that come from the work of Dr. Aaron Beck, known for his research creating cognitive behavioral therapy, and my training in resilience, which began in graduate school as a student under renowned resilience researcher and psychologist Dr. Karen Reivich, coauthor of *The Resilience Factor*.

Self-coaching can help you figure out which values drive your guilt. To illustrate, let's use the simple example of the false guilt I felt every time I went on an overnight trip. That guilt felt like a wet blanket that extinguished the fire of enthusiasm and joy the opportunity offered. Guilt-inducing thoughts created a persistent anxiety that grew each time I thought of home. I had thoughts such as these:

- *You should be at home.*
- *It's wrong for you to travel overnight when your son is so young.*
- *Your family should come before your work.*

You can imagine that with just these three condemning thoughts, even the most successful speaking engagement—during which I inspired thousands of women, spent less than twenty-four hours away from home, and arranged for my mother to spend the night at my house to help normalize my son's home environment—could lead to feelings of guilt. But I peeled back the layers to find the value that led to these thoughts. I used powerful questions (PQs) to do it. With each thought, I asked the following PQs to drill down until I arrived at the core value:

- *What does it mean to you that _____?*
- *What's the worst part of that to you?*
- *What's so upsetting about that to you?*

When I slowed down and pondered these questions, I was able to identify a value that I needed to adjust.

When you try this yourself, choose one guilty thought to start with. Then ask the questions based on just one thought at a time. I started with the thought that felt most persistent, the refrain that left me feeling the worst: *It's wrong for you to travel overnight when your son is so young.* Here is what the process looked like. Take note that it is not a perfect process. I had multiple answers to each question, which is normal. I drilled down on just one answer at a time—the answer that resonated most. Take a look.

What is so upsetting about the fact that you are "traveling overnight when your son is so young"?

It means my son won't see me for twenty-four to thirty-six hours, depending on when I leave or arrive and his school schedule. It means I'll miss him and he'll probably miss me. It means my son does not have a mom who is 100 percent at home, so I have to rely on others to fill in the gap.

What does it mean to you that you have to rely on others to fill in the gap? What's the worst part of that to you?

The worst part of it is that it makes me feel selfish. Maybe my absence will cause him anxiety. Maybe it means I am failing. I am falling short as a mother because I don't have enough time to fulfill my commitments.

Now you might be objecting, *What does Valorie mean by "when he's so young"? How young is too young for a mother to travel overnight? Why does it matter if his mom is 100 percent at home? Is she doing something wrong if she isn't?*

If you began questioning the validity or relevance of how I stated some of my thoughts, you are on to something. This is what building thought awareness is all about. Some of what we say is based on false assumptions and even faulty information. Until we slow down and articulate our thoughts, it is easy not to notice what exactly we are saying to ourselves and how it impacts our guilt.

Push Back: Is That Thought True?

The next part of this process is essential for letting go of the guilt. I call it "pushing back." Some of your thoughts are honest, but they are not necessarily the truth.

In my case, I honestly thought, *You should be at home.* Notice the verb *should*, a classic guilt word. Also notice the broad vagueness of the statement. In order to let go of my guilt, I had to push back on this persistent thought. Pushing back means asking questions that help you decide if a thought is true, and if it is, under what circumstances. You could ask questions such as these:

- *Is this true?*
- *According to whom?*
- *Why is this true? Why is it not true?*
- *If it is true, why is it important to me? If it isn't true, why is it important that I stop embracing this lie?*
- *If it isn't true as I have stated it, under what circumstances might it be true for me?*

When I pushed back whether the thought *You should be at home* was true, my answer was, *Not when I have work to do that requires me to leave home overnight. However, as much as possible, I want to be home. My family life takes a higher priority than my work in this season of life, so I must be very discerning about what opportunities I take on. This will allow me to be at peace and guilt-free when I decide to travel overnight.*

By pushing back on a thought, I found the grain of truth in that thought: *I want to be home as much as possible.* Why? I want to savor as many moments, teach as many lessons, have as much fun, and create as many beautiful memories as I can. My work lets me fulfill my calling and contribute to my family in a way that allows my husband and me to live the life we believe God has called us to. That life may look different from yours, but I am clear that I am doing what I am meant to be doing in this season.

As I reflected on the thoughts I wrote, I felt a conviction strengthen in me. Answering these simple but powerful questions forced me to clarify my values. And once clarified, I could own them! I could articulate what was true for me in a way I had not done before.

Each time you articulate a thought that causes guilt, ask a simple but powerful question: *Is that true?* If it is not, correct yourself. In my case, I had to ask myself, *Under what circumstances would it be bad to travel overnight without my baby?* Amazingly, I had never actually pondered that question. I am not even sure I realized I was thinking it until I answered the questions to uncover my values. *Well,* I thought, *if I were breastfeeding, I'd probably want to avoid travel if I could. Or if I'd just had the baby and the doctor advised against it. I would not be okay with traveling overnight if I didn't have someone I was comfortable with who was keeping my son. For me, that means a trusted family member. But most of the time, Jeff and our two other children (my bonus daughters) are there if I'm gone. When they're all home, Alex doesn't even miss me, to be honest. And if Jeff isn't home, then my mother spends the night, which Alex sees as a big, wonderful treat. He loves for Grandmommy to come over.*

And with that, I found my value statement: It is not wrong for me to travel overnight. I have given a lot of thought to the circumstances under which I am comfortable traveling overnight, and I spend a lot of time arranging those circumstances. I do not believe it is harmful to Alex. And my needing to travel is part of our family's reality. In some ways, it has even helped my son become more flexible and independent.

Each time you articulate a thought that causes guilt, ask a simple but powerful question: *Is that true?*

Do you see how that works? Stopping for a moment to ask powerful questions helps you peel back the layers to discover what you actually believe. Otherwise, self-sabotaging thoughts that are not even true can create feelings of guilt that drain your joy. Are you willing to do the work of building awareness of your thoughts so you can intentionally choose your values?

Own Your Values

There is such power in owning your values. You are, in essence, saying, "This is what I believe, and I am going to live my life according to my beliefs. I understand if you don't hold the same beliefs and values, but these are mine."

How do you start owning your values? The first step, which we've begun above, is identifying what your values are. That takes some self-reflection. Most people do not intentionally identify their values. Instead, most of us live by our values without actually stating what they are. If I could watch a recording of your life over the last seven days, I could tell you exactly what your values are. How you spend your time shows what matters most to you, what you prioritize, and what you do (and don't do). But the beauty of intentionally identifying your values is that it is a declaration, a stake in the ground that says, "This is what I am about. This is what I believe and, therefore, what I do."

For several years, Patricia questioned her dedication to her daughters when her mother expressed disapproval of her and her husband's equal-partnership approach to parenting. But one day, she finally paused to notice her thoughts about it. That's when she realized her values in this area are simply different from her mother's—and Patricia was okay with that.

When you take a stand and reject guilt for things you know are right for you, you own your values. When you find yourself feeling defensive or guilty about something because someone else thinks it's what you should do, but you don't, pause and examine your thoughts. Use the PEEL process to uncover the truth about your own values. It looks like this:

- **PINPOINT YOUR GUILT TRIGGER:** What do you feel guilty about because of others' values, or because you're trying to live by values that aren't necessarily your own? For example, Patricia's mother made disapproving comments toward her about her husband getting the kids ready in the morning.
- **EXAMINE YOUR THOUGHTS:** What do you feel like you're doing wrong? What harm did you cause? Do your thoughts line up with your values of right and wrong—or

someone else's? For example, in Patricia's case, the value was, "Mothers do the childrearing, especially when the children are girls." But that was her mother's value, not Patricia's. Patricia's was "In our home, both parents are hands-on and share the responsibility."

- **EXCHANGE THE LIE FOR THE TRUTH:** In the case of values, what you're letting go of is not necessarily a lie as much as it is a value that's not true for you. You exchange the value that is creating false guilt for the value that is your own.

- **LIST YOUR EVIDENCE:** Your evidence, when it comes to your values, is your "why" and "from where." Why does this value mean so much to you? Where does this value come from? Does it align with your faith? Your beliefs? List your evidence, and you will naturally own your values.

Too few of us own our values. We leave decisions up to what everybody else believes rather than honestly and courageously clarifying what we believe and why, and then standing on those beliefs as we choose how we are going to live our lives. Doing so is empowering and freeing. Don't miss it!

Slow down and really get this. Take a deep breath. Pray for clarity and courage. And then watch the confidence that comes in truly becoming who you are—because you are a woman who understands her values, her expectations of herself, her boundaries with others, and the power of her God to move when she operates in faith instead of fear.

When you finally clarify and own your values, you eliminate the tendency to second-guess your choices. That's because you've decided to own your choices by understanding the values behind them. There's no need to put yourself on trial anymore. You can live your life knowing you are doing what you are meant to be doing. You've prayerfully chosen your values, and even when others judge or you don't fit in, you no longer feel guilty.

What to Do Next

Take a look at your guilt list and choose the guilt dilemma that is most persistent. Answer the following questions.

- *What is the value that makes me feel guilty?*
- *Is this true?*
- *According to whom?*
- *Why is this true? Why is it not true?*
- *If it is true, why is it important to me? If it isn't true, why is it important that I stop embracing this lie?*
- *If it isn't true as I have stated it, under what circumstances might it be true for me?*

The Upside of Guilt

Why the Traits That Make You Feel Guilty Also Make You Successful

- What good is guilt?
- How has your guilt helped you?
- Is your conscience driving your conscientiousness?

In all my searching to understand guilt, one piece of research really blew me away. I've always tended to lump guilt with negative emotions, so I was intrigued to discover that neuroscience research shows that our brains actually reward us for feeling guilt. Guilt, along with its cousins pride and shame, activates neural circuits that are considered the reward centers in your brain, according to Dr. Alex Korb, a neuroscientist and author of *Upward Spiral*.[1] Because guilt can be triggered by even trivial matters that still light up the brain's rewards centers, it can be addictive. This may explain why we enjoy others' confessions. We think, *Well, at least I'm not* that *bad*, and we feel just a little bit better. We realize we are not alone in our guilt. We might even revel in it, at times, when we joke and brag about our mess-ups and shortcomings. Social media is full of guilt-filled memes and posts about parenting mishaps and romantic frustrations, work musings and exercise goals gone bad. There is a sort of camaraderie in failed expectations. "Oh, it's not just me! It's you too! Aren't we amazing . . . not!"

But why would guilt be rewarded with feel-good chemicals? The thinking is that guilt can drive good behavior. It is an incentive to do what is right and moral, to be fair and treat others well.[2]

If you've been beating yourself up about feeling guilty, it's a welcome message to know there might be a positive side to your guilt. Even though your feelings of guilt might at times be draining, they might also have contributed to your success, your relationships, and the good decisions you've made. That's because guilt serves a purpose besides torturing us with negative feelings. Ultimately, it motivates us to improve our behavior, do the right things, and do right by others.

There's a prominent belief that successful people are successful because they've tapped into their passion and love what they do. The idea is that if you like something, you'll be naturally driven and committed to it. But what if that's just a small piece of the puzzle? What if that gives too much credit to the power of positive emotion to motivate us and not enough credit to the positive power of negative emotion?

For example, guilt may play a stronger role in your attendance record at work than how much you love what you do. One study sought to determine the correlation between job satisfaction and work attendance. The assumption was that employees who enjoy their jobs are more likely to show up for work every day, and that those who are dissatisfied are more likely to have higher rates of absenteeism. Makes sense, right? But it turns out the assumption was faulty. Rebecca Schaumberg, assistant professor at the Wharton School at the University of Pennsylvania, and Francis Flynn, professor of organizational behavior at Stanford Graduate School of Business, published their findings about the role of guilt proneness in employee reliability in the *Journal of Applied Psychology*. They define "guilt proneness" as the employee's "tendency to experience negative feelings about personal wrongdoing."[3] They found that those who were more guilt prone tended to show up for work at high rates regardless of whether they were satisfied with their jobs. Those who were less guilt prone showed up at high rates only if they liked their jobs. Schaumberg and Flynn have found similar results in a variety of industries, from customer service call centers to agriculture and entertainment.

These reliable employees are motivated by meeting the "normative expectations" of others above fulfilling their own immediate interests, according to the researchers. In other words, norms drive guilt-prone people. Another simple word for norms is *expectations*. And you may remember that guilt is often driven by the feeling that you have not lived up to expectations— whether you set them or others did. Success in the workplace often has to do with upholding the expectations the organization has put in place as their norm. Schaumberg and Flynn's studies of guilt-prone individuals have shown other positive outcomes as well, including receiving higher ratings on performance reviews and being seen as capable individuals who are more committed to the organizations for which they work.

These guilt-prone workers may be more committed to good deeds too. In an interview with *Harvard Business Review*, Flynn acknowledged, "They may be more selfless as well. We see a strong connection between guilt tendencies and altruistic behavior. The guilty are more willing to make charitable contributions and assist colleagues in need. There seems to be a link between guilt and positive social behavior."[4]

The focus of my work over the years has been to study and teach what successful women do differently. I believe wholeheartedly that too many of us focus too much on the steps to success and not enough on the thought process of success. The prevailing idea is that if you know the steps, you can get to the finish line of any goal. But this idea misses critical information. Along your journey, you are bound to face obstacles, disappointments, or setbacks. The difference between those who are successful and those who are average or unsuccessful is what they say to themselves every step along the journey. What do they say to themselves when setting a goal? What do they say when faced with doubt? What do they say when they fail? When they are wrong? When they get embarrassed? When a key relationship goes south? The most successful women don't just follow certain steps; they think differently in the face of every challenge and opportunity they face. The assumption might be that their thoughts are all positive, but that's not true. While I never would have thought it prior to diving into the research on guilt, guilt plays a role in their success.

There are many upsides to guilt, one of which is that the *anticipation of guilt* can guide your behavior in such a way that it makes you more trustworthy and successful. It can lead to self-control in situations where you'd rather give up (like when you want to hit snooze and call in sick). It can cause you to uphold the goals of your employer and look out for their best interests (which can lead to promotions, recognition, and raises). It can cause you to give to those in need (a habit that leads to happiness and fulfillment). So while it can appear that guilt is a negative emotion that always steals our joy, the anticipation of guilt if we don't live up to expectations can actually lead us to make choices that meet others' expectations. And those choices often come with positive rewards and success. This is the upside of guilt: it can be a guide that makes you better. For example:

- **GUILT PROMPTS YOU TO DO THE RIGHT THING.** Over time, doing the right thing builds positive relationships, helps you reach important goals, and makes you trustworthy.
- **GUILT HELPS YOU STAY TRUE TO YOUR VALUES.** Staying true to your values brings peace. It also means being authentic, a necessary skill for resilience.
- **GUILT IS AN INVITATION TO TAKE RESPONSIBILITY.** It's healthy to own up to it when you are wrong. Guilt invites you to take responsibility for your actions.
- **GUILT CAN TRIGGER POSITIVE CHANGE.** If you want to align your actions with your values and be at peace, then guilt, or the anticipation of it, can motivate you to take action to change.
- **GUILT CONTROLS GREED.** Guilt can trigger fairness when excesses tip out of balance.

One of the most fascinating connections between success and guilt is related to one particular personality trait that is common among highly successful individuals.

The Success Trait That Breeds Guilt

The *anticipation of guilt* can guide your behavior in such a way that it makes you more trustworthy and successful.

In psychology, researchers have pinpointed five personality traits as common categories for us all, often referred to as the "big five personality traits." According to researchers, personality traits are "defined as relatively enduring patterns of thoughts, feelings, and behaviors that represent a readiness to respond in particular ways to specific environmental cues."[5] The five personality traits are

- openness
- conscientiousness
- extroversion
- neuroticism
- agreeableness

Among them all, one in particular is most common among highly successful individuals: conscientiousness. "Conscientiousness is the tendency to be planful, organized, task- and goal-oriented, and self-controlled, and to delay gratification and follow norms and rules."[6] The *Oxford English Dictionary* defines *conscientiousness* as the quality of wishing to do one's work or duty well and thoroughly.[7] Here are a few other qualities that define conscientious people:

- hardworking
- dependable

- diligent
- organized
- careful
- dutiful
- deliberate
- thorough
- achievement oriented

What are some clues a person is conscientious? Someone who maintains to-do lists, planners and well-kept calendars, neatly organized bookshelves and closets, strong attendance at work or school, regular doctor visits, and even deliberate spending habits may be a conscientious person. This is certainly not an exhaustive list by any stretch, but the point here is that conscientious people tend to engage in behaviors that are efficient, consider future consequences, and enable them to succeed at reaching positive outcomes.

In fact, reading and listening to books that help you grow and achieve goals is a conscientious behavior. I'm not saying this is your primary personality trait, but my guess is that you may relate at least somewhat to it. After all, you could spend your time doing something that takes much less focus and drive than reading a book about how to overcome one of your life's challenges, right? Those lacking in this trait tend to be less concerned about goals and more laid back.

Conscientiousness and Guilt

So how does all of this relate to guilt? Conscientious people believe they are doing their work well and fulfilling their duties and obligations—or at least aiming to. They are acting responsibly. They are working hard. They are upholding norms. They are living up to others' expectations. They are exercising self-control and sacrificing in the present in order to get what they want in the future. These behaviors are what a conscientious person values as virtuous—behaviors that lead to a future that is well planned and rewarded by thoughtfulness and deliberation.

It makes sense that conscientious people are successful for many reasons. Conscientious people behave in ways that display order, industriousness, responsibility, impulse control, and conventionality.[8] Researchers go on to explain that those who are conscientious "tend to organize their lives, work hard to achieve goals, meet the expectations of others, avoid giving in to temptations, and uphold norms and rules of life more than others."[9] Read that last sentence closely, and you'll notice that these tendencies create a setup to fall short of expectations sometimes. Goals, temptations, norms, and rules all require self-control. And the truth is, self-control is a limited resource. If you need it constantly, you are bound to run out—and that's when guilt sets in. And yet, looking at this description, you can also see why many leaders, star athletes, and highly educated individuals are conscientious. Reaching high levels of success requires the planning, perseverance, and self-control marked by conscientiousness.

If guilt comes from falling short of expectations, and conscientiousness results in meeting or exceeding expectations, then it seems the conscientious person would feel guilt-free and full of joy, right? They are dutiful and thorough—and this aligns with their values, which feels good. As a result, it seems they'd experience less guilt than other personality types, not more.

But perhaps it is because conscientiousness leads a person to uphold norms, strive to succeed, and live up to others' expectations that they end up experiencing more opportunity to fall short. It's hard to keep it up all the time. And when they don't, it feels like they are doing something wrong, which leads to guilt. Here's why:

- "Norms" are basically rules for what is acceptable. They are expectations driven by values that the conscientious person has made the decision to embrace. Remember that guilt is based on your values and the expectations that emerge from those values. Upholding norms is a behavior driven by guilt, because a conscientious person sees norms as the right thing to do.
- Living up to others' expectations is an other-focused goal. And as I mentioned earlier, guilt is an other-focused emotion. It ensues when we feel we have somehow caused harm. Letting others down by not meeting their expectations creates guilt when we feel we have caused harm by doing so.
- Because we are human, imperfection is inevitable. When a conscientious person falls short, they feel they have done something wrong. If they were just a bit more careful, thoughtful, or self-controlled, they suppose, maybe they wouldn't have messed up. The inability to perfectly maintain such high standards creates higher feelings of guilt, especially false guilt in conscientious individuals.

Consider Kara, for example. She recently launched a business as a relationship coach after going through our coach training program. A very conscientious person, Kara diligently followed the business development plan she learned in our program. She was careful to carve out time to build her side business so it didn't interfere with her performance at her main job. She was doing everything she learned during her professional training—she was clear about her target audience, was diligent about learning her craft, and had begun marketing discreetly in order to avoid any raised eyebrows from her employer. Her work as a coach was unrelated to her full-time job as a corporate trainer, but she didn't want it to appear she was not giving her all on the job or had lost her focus. In the last six months, she had picked up a total of four weekly clients, whom she coached on Tuesday evenings and Saturday mornings. Things were going well, although she sometimes wished the business would take off a little faster. She'd ultimately love to take the entrepreneurial leap out of her corporate job and work for herself full time.

Last week, while scrolling her social media feed, where she follows many coaches whose success inspires her, she ended up beating herself up. After looking at what some of them were doing and how successful their businesses seemed to become in a short period of time, she was overwhelmed by guilt.

If I were more organized with my time, perhaps I would be further along. I'm only spending about eight hours per week on this business. I could do more. Maybe I'm not taking this seriously enough. I'm not working hard enough, she said to herself.

As she went through the mental checklist of marketing activities and ideas that she had not yet implemented, her guilt grew. After just six months of building her business, perhaps her guilt was unwarranted, but her conscientiousness set high expectations for a work schedule that would have been nearly impossible for her to meet in the time she'd had.

Be Conscientious About the Right Thing

While conscientiousness leads to carrying out responsibilities and duties effectively, it is possible to be conscientious about the wrong things. For example, norms are subjective. They represent a set of values, but whose values? Your family can have dysfunctional norms, and yet you find yourself feeling guilty when you don't conform to those norms. Likewise, you can work within an organization whose values you do not share, yet you may live up to those values because those are norms that have been declared and that get rewarded. You may find yourself feeling guilty and conflicted when you don't conform to those norms—and guilty and conflicted when you do.

You can't just be conscientious about living up to norms; you need to be conscientious about what norms are truly right and good. This is how you reset and adjust your behavior to eliminate false guilt. You must intentionally choose your norms based on your values. Own those values so you can let go of the guilt.

Instead of trying to meet others' expectations or norms as dictated by your employer, culture, or society at large, decide which expectations are right to meet. What is the ultimate right? The higher good? What are your norms? You've got to be clear.

What's normal to others may not be normal to you. Yet it can be hard to clarify and own your values when you are rewarded for living up to the values of your family, culture, or company.

What's Your Conscience Telling You?

Anita had been the advertising sales director for a multimillion dollar media company for several years when her boss informed her the business would be sold to an industry leader within a matter of months. The company wanted to continue bringing in advertising commitments for the upcoming quarters but didn't want clients to find out about the sale. The problem was, with the sale of their stations, the entire format would be changed, which meant the targeted audience would change. Many clients would reconsider their ad buys if they were aware of the impending sale. After all, they were advertising to a specific audience, which Anita and her sales team would continue to promote as though nothing was about to change. Anita was very conscientious and had made millions for the company, but she also had a conscience.

"I considered many of these clients my friends," she recalled. "I'd worked with them at previous jobs, and they trusted me. To pretend I didn't know about the sale and allow them to spend money knowing they would not get what they thought they were buying was just wrong." But most on her team went along with the plan. Anita had a choice to make—lie to her clients in order to make sales, or lose her job. She chose the latter.

In essence, the anticipation of guilt from knowing that she would be lying to clients kept her from acting against her values. Anita knew what her values were, and misleading people and manipulating situations to her benefit at the expense of others did not fit. Nonetheless, those were the norms and expectations of her employer.

Other coworkers stayed and lived up to those norms and

expectations. "I don't know if they felt guilt about lying. But once the company was purchased, they lost their jobs anyway," she remembered. "The new owner wanted new people. That's how it always is."

Anita's dilemma was an opportunity to own her values, even if it meant giving up her job. Because of her reputation as a conscientious leader with a conscience, she quickly landed a new position at another company doing similar work she enjoyed.

The Gift of Guilt

If you are conscientious, you can be relied upon to carry out certain responsibilities with consistency. If you are guided by your conscience, you can be relied upon to carry out what is *right* with consistency. Your conscience is what makes your conscientiousness truly powerful. This combination leads to authentic success. The woman who owns her values has both conscientiousness and a conscience.

When viewed through the lens of conscience, guilt—or the anticipation of it—is a gift. It is the gift that enables you to align your values and beliefs with your actions. Doing this, especially when your ethics and morality could come into question, is essential. While conscientiousness is about doing things well and meeting expectations, when those expectations are immoral, conscientiousness is no longer the answer. Conscience is.

Conscientiousness without conscience is dangerous. On a societal level, it has caused some of history's greatest injustices and atrocities. It's how the Holocaust happened. It's how segregation and Jim Crow were maintained. On a personal level, it is also detrimental. You don't want to be merely conscientious; you want to have a purpose. Your conscientiousness must be guided by a higher authority. Your conscience is your moral compass, your guide. For me, that guide is the Holy Spirit. It is a voice of God Himself nudging me in the right direction.

If you are a woman of faith, your beliefs define your values. When I open my Bible, I'm clear about what matters. It's not something I make up. It's there in clear print. And sometimes it requires the humility of understanding the state of all human beings—that we are all guilty, that none of us is perfect. Jesus illustrated this point so profoundly in the gospel of John in the New Testament when he challenged those who were ready to stone a woman to death who had been caught in the act of adultery. He said to them, "'He that is without sin among you, let him first cast a stone at her.' And again he stooped down, and wrote on the ground. And they which heard it, being convicted by their own conscience, went out one by one" (John 8:7–9 KJV).

His words spoke to the conscience of each person in the crowd that day. Ego is prideful, even judgmental, but the conscience is humble. When you act out of your conscience, good guilt emerges—guilt that is rooted in truth, humble in action, and therefore primed for forgiveness.

The fact that you struggle with guilt is not a negative trait. It means you have a conscience. And your conscience has served you well. I want to help you distinguish between good guilt—the kind that makes you a better human and strengthens your relationships—and false guilt, the kind that twists a narrative, causing you to feel guilty when you are not guilty. That's toxic guilt. So as we move on, I'll give more tools to put in your toolbox so you can better navigate guilt and take back your joy.

What to Do Next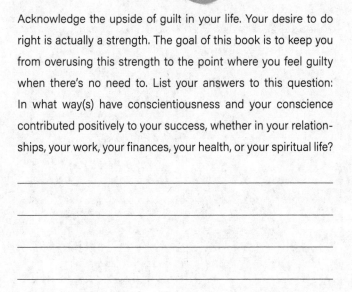

Acknowledge the upside of guilt in your life. Your desire to do right is actually a strength. The goal of this book is to keep you from overusing this strength to the point where you feel guilty when there's no need to. List your answers to this question: In what way(s) have conscientiousness and your conscience contributed positively to your success, whether in your relationships, your work, your finances, your health, or your spiritual life?

_____

_____

_____

_____

SEVEN

(Re)Set Your Expectations

Stop Setting Yourself Up for Guilt and Set Yourself Up for Happiness

- What are the ways you set yourself up for guilt?
- What expectations could you adjust?
- What will you do to reset your expectations?

Perhaps one of the reasons guilt is on the rise is because expectations have risen. Information is more abundant, and we have far more points of comparison of what we "should" be doing in our lives. Until the 1990s, if you wanted to find information, you had to go seek it out. Today, information is pushed to us. In fact, the more you read about a topic online, the more articles show up on that particular topic. It's easy to become hyperaware of what perfection supposedly looks like, and that can become your expectation about what your life "should" look like.

One of the telltale signs of an expectation that leads to guilt is the word *should*. Notice whenever you use it in everyday conversation. Those who feel guilty often say "I should . . ." or "I should have . . ." as they begin a sentence. It makes sense the two are connected, as *should* is described as a word "used to indicate obligation, duty, or correctness, typically when criticizing someone's actions."[1] Of course, guilt is about failing to meet obligation and duties, and doing things wrong. Whenever you find yourself using *should*, consider replacing it with the word *could*. *Could* communicates the message while acknowledging your choice. "I could" and "I could have" are not about obligation, but choice. So, "I should have done more" becomes "I could have done more." "I should go to this neighborhood party I don't want to go to" becomes "I could go to this neighborhood party I don't want to go to." A shift in your words can create a shift in your thoughts.

There is no guilt without expectation. And so there is no faster way to undo your guilty feelings than to adjust your expectations of yourself. To do that, you must first pay attention. That means slowing down and examining your expectations under a microscope. Sometimes our expectations are so vague we never feel like we've done enough to meet them. Other times, our expectations aren't even ours; instead, they are the rules and norms that don't align with our values. And sometimes our expectations are outdated. They made sense in another season of our lives, but not today, not with the vision and responsibilities we now have.

> Sometimes our expectations are outdated. They made sense in another season of our lives, but not today.

To let go of guilt, we must let go of expectations that do not align with who and where we are and reset our expectations intentionally to reflect the joy and purpose we so deeply want. This takes self-compassion. Rather than beating yourself up for falling short of misguided expectations, instead be kind to yourself for trying so hard to meet those expectations. Then take a breath. Pivot. Decide whether those expectations are the right ones for you to have.

So much of the journey we are taking through these pages is about waking up to the thoughts that create feelings of guilt, then consciously choosing new thoughts. These new thoughts create new feelings. Most people don't pay attention to their thoughts in this way. They simply allow whatever thoughts come to mind to lead them. But to live a life of freedom and joy, thought awareness isn't an option. It has to be a daily habit.

Expectations are thoughts about what you *should* be doing. An expectation is an agreement you make with yourself about what you will and will not do. To conquer guilt, you must consciously and intentionally set the expectations you have of yourself. If you don't, it's likely you'll set yourself up for guilt without even realizing that's what you're doing. In this chapter, let's talk about five types of expectations that set you up for guilt and how to spot them. Then you will learn how to reset your expectations to create clarity, peace, and joy.

Expectations differ from values in that values are what matter most to you—what you deem most important. Expectations are what you believe you should or should not do as a result of those values. So if one of your values is freedom, you might have an expectation that you should be conservative with your spending or aggressive about earning more money because you believe doing so will bring financial freedom. If you have a value of creativity, you may have an expectation that your kids' birthday parties should be themed, planned, and unique expressions of their personalities. Or you feel that your presentations at work should never use a cookie-cutter template but instead have a special and memorable design that takes more time and effort to pull together.

Vague Expectations

Perhaps the most persistent and elusive of expectations is the vague expectation—for example, *You should do more.* Well, how much is more? And what should you "do" exactly? Without specifics, you never know when you've done enough. So the vague expectation sets you up for guilt because you can't really measure whether you've met the expectation. And if you tend to be hard on yourself, you'll never think you've done enough.

Ericka showed up for her coaching session beating herself up terribly. She had a long guilt list, and the two things at the top of her list were about not spending enough time with two loved ones who were in a vulnerable position.

"I feel very guilty that I live in a different city than my brother and I don't see him often enough," she explained. Her brother had been disabled in an accident in his twenties, and while he can function and live alone, he still had many challenges. Ericka promised her mother before she died that she would always make sure her brother was taken care of, and while she had done that, she felt she wasn't living up to that expectation the way she would like.

"I make sure he has what he needs financially, I talk to him a couple of times a day, and other family members stop by a couple of times a week," she went on. "But I'm not there. And moving here would be too hard on him. It's too much change."

"Do you think your mother would be disappointed?" I

asked. "Have you somehow not taken care of your brother and let her down?"

Ericka paused and sighed. "Well, I've taken care of him, but I think she'd want me closer to him." But, though it was the long-term plan, she couldn't do that yet because it wasn't financially feasible. So she visited when she could.

But it wasn't just the situation with her brother that had her feeling guilty. Her aunt was ill and elderly, and Ericka hadn't seen her in nearly a year. "It's a five-hour drive, and we have just been too busy lately. My husband has been traveling a lot, so trying to find a weekend when we can make the drive has been nearly impossible," she explained. "But I feel so guilty about it. She is my last living aunt—the only one left in my parents' generation on both sides. She's in a nursing home. I just want her to feel loved and to know I care."

As I listened to Ericka talk about her guilt, I had two goals: (1) help her clarify whether she was experiencing authentic guilt or false guilt, and (2) help her let go of the guilt and take actions that bring feelings of joy in these relationships that are so dear to her. To do that, we would need to peel back the layers of expectations that had left Ericka beating herself up daily. It wasn't always a conscious berating, but rather lingering sad thoughts that she was disappointing her late mother, failing her brother, and neglecting her beloved aunt. Although she had not specifically called her thoughts "expectations," that is exactly what they were. And the expectations were so relentless that even when she did spend time with her brother or call her aunt, she still had an abiding feeling that she was not doing enough.

The process I guided Ericka through is the same process we can all use to peel back the layers of thoughts and emotions that make it so hard to let go of guilt. The process revealed that her thoughts centered around expectations she had not yet examined and articulated. It looked like this:

ME: In a single sentence, what are you guilty of exactly?

ERICKA: Not being there enough for my brother the way I promised I would be. And not being there and honoring my aunt in her old age.

ME: Okay, let's start with the first accusation, not being there for your brother. How do you define "being there"?

ERICKA: I would cook him a home-cooked meal every once in a while. That's all he ever asks for when I come. He never gets a home-cooked meal. I feel so badly about that.

ME: How often would you have to cook him a meal in order to feel that you were there enough for your brother?

I want to stop here for a moment to point out why I am asking these questions. When we feel guilty, it can be very easy to mention expectations we are not meeting without ever *defining* those expectations. In this case, Ericka felt guilty that she was not there enough for her brother. It is a refrain she repeated often and for years, not just in passing during coaching sessions but to friends and family members, and most damaging, to herself almost daily. And yet, when I asked her how often she'd need to be there in order to meet the expectation, she said she'd never asked that question of herself.

How often do we do that to ourselves? We set an expectation

that has no clear definition or boundaries—*I should do more for my kids, spend more time with my family, work harder, exercise more*—and then beat ourselves up for falling short. But without a quantifiable goal, when have you done enough? The answer is, you have no idea. You've never done enough. There's always more you could do. So let's peel back the layers of this problem.

1. Pinpoint your guilt trigger.

I call this your "guilty statement." Articulate a sentence that describes your guilt trigger and the reason it creates feelings of guilt. In Ericka's case, her guilty statement was, "I feel guilty about not being there enough for my brother the way I promised I would be. And not being there and honoring my aunt in her old age."

NARROW THE GUILT TRIGGER TO JUST ONE CHALLENGE AT A TIME. Ericka identified two things she felt guilty about, but we could only address one at a time. So we narrowed it. When you limit yourself to one specific thought, you can pinpoint your feelings about it. Attempting to talk about multiple dilemmas simultaneously makes it more difficult to create a breakthrough. You will instead find yourself speaking in broad terms, and broad isn't a target you can successfully aim for.

2. Examine your thoughts (define the expectation).

"How do you define 'being there'?" I asked Ericka. This is critical. "Being there" is vague, and we all define it differently. Ericka seemed to define being there as cooking for him, but she didn't specify how often. So I followed up with the question, "How often would you have to cook him a meal in order to feel you were there enough for your brother?" The goal here is to get as specific as possible about the expectation, because it is the expectation that sets you up for success or failure, joy or guilt.

Let's take a look at what she said in answer to that question.

> ERICKA: I would go visit every three months for three days over a weekend.
>
> ME: Okay, so if you visited him every three months and cooked for him while you were there, you would feel you were there enough for him?
>
> ERICKA: Yes, I would feel good about that.
>
> ME: And how often are you seeing him now?
>
> ERICKA: Well, let me think. We went for his birthday, Christmas, Thanksgiving, my son's birthday, and two other trips in the last year. So six times. But they weren't all trips just to visit him.
>
> ME: So you've visited six times? Did you cook?
>
> ERICKA: Not every time, no. Twice I didn't cook.
>
> ME: So you cooked for him during four trips in the last year?
>
> ERICKA: Yes.
>
> ME: So you are already averaging the number of trips and home-cooked meals you are saying you need in order to feel you are there for him often enough. What's missing that is causing you to feel guilty?
>
> ERICKA: (*pause*) You know, I think it is that I don't have a plan for any future dates. And I feel so busy.

3. Exchange the lie for the truth.

Ericka's guilt, as you can see, was false guilt. She wasn't actually doing anything wrong. But she *felt* she was doing something wrong. In clarifying her definition of "enough," I was able to get her to see that she was already visiting more than her expectation dictated. But since she kept referencing being busy, I wanted to peel back the layer there as well to get her to commit to some future dates so that she could feel some joy and peace about plans to see her brother. In recent months, she'd traveled home for her brother's birthday, the engagement party of one of her adult children, and an event for her husband's family. She'd traveled for a weeklong vacation and twice for work. And she was expecting to travel back in a couple of months for the holidays. She usually cooked and hosted holiday dinners at her brother's, and extended family would come too.

> ME: How many weekends per month would you like to be home?
>
> ERICKA: This month, it's only one. Two would be nice.
>
> ME: Is two what you want, or is that what you'd settle for?
>
> ERICKA: What I'd settle for.
>
> ME: How many weekends at home *do you want*?
>
> ERICKA: Three would be amazing.
>
> ME: Okay, how about you aim for three? That would give you about thirteen weekends each year to travel. How many of those thirteen weekends will you commit to your brother, and how many to your aunt, in the coming year?

4. List your evidence.

As you may have noticed during the "examine your thoughts" and "exchange lies for the truth" phases of our coaching conversation, Ericka listed evidence that she had actually visited her brother six times and cooked for him four times, which met the expectations she articulated when I asked her to define the expectations. She then laid out a plan moving forward that was specific. All of this fulfilled the "list your evidence" phase of the PEEL process. It is okay if you find yourself coaching through the PEEL process to pinpoint and clarify your expectations, and the process does not occur in perfect order. The important thing is that you walk through each step of the process.

My goal was to help Ericka get specific about her expectations and set herself up to feel good about all she wants to do for the people she loves. Although we'd not transitioned into talking about her guilty feelings about not spending more time with her aunt, I knew that was a part of her vision; and since she'd clarified her goal around being there for her brother, I included her in the question.

By the end of her coaching session, Ericka said she felt as though a weight had been lifted off her shoulders. She also committed to a total of fourteen weekends away, including trips with her husband, a girlfriend trip, a birthday weekend, and weekends with her brother, aunt, and other family.

I also asked her about the other things she was doing to "be there" for her brother and aunt. It was quite a list. For example, she checked that her brother's bills were paid, talked to him multiple times a day, ensured her adult children stopped by regularly to see him, and made a big deal of his birthday and holidays. She still planned to move back eventually, and our session was an impetus to talk with her husband about a goal date to do that, even if it would be five years from now. As for her aunt, Ericka threw a big eightieth birthday party, spent every birthday with her the last few years, sent her care packages once a month, and called her at least twice a month. When Ericka lived closer she visited her aunt often, and Ericka's kids got to know their great-aunt well and have fond memories. "There's no question I have honored her and she knows I love her, even if I am not there often," Ericka admitted.

Ericka's guilt stemmed from vague expectations that she never seemed to meet. Her guilt statement was hard to dispute: "Not being there more for my brother" and "Not being there more and honoring my aunt in her old age." By defining "being there more," she could suddenly see that she had actually been meeting her own expectations, but because she had not clearly defined them, the thought that she should "be there more" overwhelmed her. There's always more you could be doing. Setting a clear expectation of when you have achieved "more" is a key to eliminating guilt.

Outdated Expectations

Expectations must be reevaluated as your circumstances change. Most people, of course, don't think to themselves, *I am entering a new season. I need to sit down and reevaluate my expectations.* But those who do have a significant advantage.

When your life changes in some way, take time to examine your expectations and reset them if needed. Whether

> There's always more you could be doing. Setting a clear expectation of when you have achieved "more" is a key to eliminating guilt.

the life change is a new job, relationship change, financial change, health change, a move, or anything else that shifts how your life operates day to day, you'll set yourself up for guilt if you hold on to old expectations in a new season. Even a change in your spiritual and emotional growth is worthy of pause. As you have worked through the concepts and coaching in this book, you've seen your perspective shift, and that warrants a review of the expectations you've previously agreed to.

The expectations that were okay in the last season may not be okay now. *And that's okay.* When you attempt to live up to outdated expectations, you block your ability to meet the fresh expectations of the season you are in. And you can be left feeling guilty about not living up to expectations that are no longer appropriate or even attainable in a new season.

For example, consider a parent who committed to helping an adult child financially during a transition from school to landing a job and becoming self-sustaining. Both parties can find themselves in a confusing place if expectations regarding a timeline were not set. What the parent intended as six to twelve months of financial help can turn into three years with no end in sight, leaving the parent feeling guilty about the idea of cutting off the assistance. The expectation that the parent would pay for certain expenses was meant for a season, and that season is over. By resetting the expectation, the parent is released from an obligation that is no longer appropriate, and the adult child is freed to step up and stand on his or her own, which is what is healthy for everyone. Even if you did not make your intentions clear at first, you can do it now.

Outdated expectations can easily occur in relationships with children because as they get older and more mature, what they are capable of and responsible for changes. This happens in other areas too; it's easy to keep doing what you've always done. Perhaps you are in a new job with a longer commute or more demanding schedule, yet you feel guilty you haven't been able to do certain things you used to do. Now you beat yourself up about not getting together with friends as often or not living up to your old expectations about housekeeping. But if you stopped and reexamined your expectations, you'd realize you may need to reset them if you are to let go of the guilt and get your joy back.

Unbalanced Expectations

Unbalanced expectations occur when you expect more of yourself than you do of others. This often happens when you feel you must compensate for your good fortune or for the debts you believe you owe by taking on responsibilities in unbalanced ways. For example, my work often takes me out of the office on trips—sometimes I speak at conferences on weekends—and my writing may require me to work when I can find quiet solitude, like 4:00 a.m. or late in the evening after everyone goes to bed. This means I may take time off during the week when the rest of my team is working. I had to let go of guilt that I was somehow being unfair to expect them to keep regular office hours when I was resting. Those were my guilt-drenched thoughts. And I often let those thoughts take control of my actions, meaning I would go into the office out of a sense of fairness rather than getting some much-deserved and needed rest. My expectations were unbalanced. I had to reset this unreasonable expectation by examining the truth behind the circumstances.

As both the creative and the entrepreneur, my role and level of responsibility is different from the rest of the team's. The expectation for me is not measured by "hours worked" or what time or day I work. It is measured by the quality and impact of the content I create and the focus, fun, and excellence with which the business is run. I applied the PEEL process to reset my expectations in this area. First, I pinpointed my guilt, which was that I was doing something wrong when I opted sometimes to rest during office hours. Then I examined that thought—the expectation that I should not rest during office hours. Next, I exchanged it for the truth: as the owner / writer / speaker / content creator, I am not obligated to keep office hours. I am obligated to fulfill my purpose and run a successful business, however much or little time that takes. No one else has that level of responsibility and obligation. It was completely unbalanced to treat office hours as sacred while not accounting for the wear and tear of my non-office hours. I believe my thinking was rooted in a set expectation pattern from the short time I worked in corporate America. When I transitioned from employee to entrepreneur, I held on to an outdated expectation in a new season, which then created unbalanced expectations that set me up for guilt.

Unbalanced expectations also show up for people who tend toward "overresponsibility." Those who are overresponsible take charge of other people's responsibilities; over time, that habit can become an unbalanced expectation. The result is that you end up feeling guilty if you don't keep it up. Sometimes you end up overresponsible purely out of fear: *They won't do it right, so I'll just do it for them.* Or self-interest: *I want Timmy to get into a great college because it is a reflection of my parenting, so I'm going to keep track of his assignments for him and email his teachers to get him extra time when he forgets assignments or turns them in late.* But many times, overresponsibility is rooted in faulty expectations that give you no grace for the challenges that affect you.

Perfectionistic Expectations

Reshma Saujani, founder of Girls Who Code, said in her famous TED Talk that "we as a culture raise our boys to be brave and our girls to be perfect."[2] This is largely true. Perfectionism is largely a women's issue, and that has to do with how we are socialized. We should look pretty, we should be neat, we should find a fairytale husband and have well-behaved children. We should have the perfect home and home decor, the perfect meals, and the perfect body. These are the messages we get over and over and over again. No wonder we have so much anxiety and stress! Even when we don't want to, it can be so easy to internalize these expectations and make them our own.

Culturally, there is a reward for being perfect: adoration praise, approval, and acceptance rather than rejection. But letting go of guilt means letting go of certain expectations. That is a risk. It is the risk of not being accepted or embraced. It is the risk of imperfection. If perfection guarantees approval and acceptance, it's always going to be hard to let go of. The question is, whose acceptance matters to you?

One of the most toxic expectations is the self-imposed expectation of perfectionism. The symptoms are defensiveness, comparison, and harsh words directed at yourself. You freely beat yourself up for your perceived imperfections, but if you think others might notice those imperfections, you are defensive in your response. Since you're already beating yourself up, you don't need others pointing out your flaws too. The thing is, though, others often are not criticizing you when you feel criticized. You just interpret it that way because of your own frustration with your inability to consistently live up to your self-imposed expectations of perfection.

I know this one well because I have lived it. It is one of the areas I discovered and conquered while researching guilt. It showed up for me as defensiveness. A close friend asked me why I had been defensive about some questions she asked me. (Nothing like a good friend to call you out on your stuff!) Her question confused me at first because I thought it was obvious why I was defensive. She was trying to help me figure out the best way to move forward with a project, and rather than give me advice, she kept asking me questions I didn't have answers to. With each question, I was reminded of how much I didn't know that I felt I should know. Didn't she know I didn't know? Why'd she need to point it out by asking questions I couldn't answer? I felt exposed and flooded with feelings that I was failing and incompetent. Pretty harsh.

Her intention was just the opposite—to get me to think about some possible answers, not feel guilty for not knowing them. That's when I decided to examine my thoughts. What self-imposed expectation was creating these feelings of guilt? Perfectionism. We were discussing something related to my work, and my expectation was that I would know all the answers. I had a fixed mind-set and didn't even realize it. A fixed mind-set believes that your intelligence, talent, and abilities are fixed and immovable, not something you can improve through effort but set traits that you either have or don't have.[3]

By admitting my defensiveness, I discovered something about myself: I had an expectation of myself that set me up for guilt. I needed to be perfect to be acceptable, and one way I defined that was knowing the answers when it came to my work. When I fell short, it meant I'd done something wrong—I'd not worked hard enough and, therefore, didn't deserve the opportunities I had.

If I expect that I'm supposed to know everything, I'll feel guilty when I don't know. When my friend asked a question I couldn't answer, it felt like she was shining a light on what I was doing wrong that I was already beating myself up for: *I don't know because I didn't take the time to figure it out myself. I don't know because I'm lazy! I haven't worked hard enough. I need to focus more.*

I was pretty shocked at what came up when I used the PEEL process to examine my thoughts. For me, defensiveness tipped me off, but remember that comparison and harsh words are also signs. Here's another example.

Sophia closed her eyes as she inhaled the sweet aroma of the strawberry buttercream icing clustered in a puff atop the scrumptious strawberry cupcake she'd picked up from her favorite little cupcakery on the way home. Savoring the sugary smell was her ritual before biting into her favorite, delectable treat. She sat in the car and ate it slowly, her taste buds reveling in the flavors and textures as the smooth, creamy icing blended with the moist cupcake. After a stressful day, it was a delightful moment of mouth-watering joy.

But almost as soon as she had swallowed the last bite of her cupcake, she felt a pang in the pit of her stomach. It wasn't cramps from the sugar. It was her emotions—disappointment with herself, followed almost immediately by guilt at doing precisely the opposite of what she'd said she'd do this week: cut out sweets in an effort to eat healthier. The negative self-talk was berating.

I promised myself this week would be the week I was finally going to start eating healthy. And look at me: gobbling up a five-hundred-calorie cupcake while still sitting in my car, no less, so no one sees what I'm up to. I just wanted a little piece of happiness after a long, hectic day. Why can't I de-stress by exercising like my health-nut coworker Angela? Why can't I be more disciplined like my sister? Ugh.

Sophia sighed as she dropped her head in frustration.

I guess I'll start next week, she told herself, only half believing it.

Comparison and harsh words toward herself were the signs pointing to Sophia's expectation of perfectionism. When I set out to write this book, I thought the biggest culprits were guilt about parenting and work and dealing with guilt trips by close friends or family members. But I was surprised to learn from surveying hundreds of women that while those areas of life definitely create a lot of guilty feelings, guilt about eating habits topped the list (followed closely by guilt about exercise habits).

And since eating is something you do multiple times every day, it leaves a lot of opportunity to feel guilty. Perhaps you've never thought of it as guilt, or never considered how the conversation in your head about what you should or shouldn't eat zaps your happiness, but it can. And here's the thing: we are bombarded with so much information about what we should eat and what we shouldn't. It exacerbates the problem, especially if you tend to be a perfectionist. Today you can have a Bluetooth scale that links to your smartwatch that tells you how much you weigh and how many steps you've taken, and beckons you to enter everything you eat into an app. That's great for goal setting and staying on track—and also great for seeing exactly how you fall short.

When you make a decision to lighten up, to have the opportunity to enjoy a treat sometimes, you can melt that guilt. According to research from the Gallup Organization, one of the best ways to improve your eating habits is to follow a very simple rule: make more good food choices than bad ones.[4] If food is a guilt trigger for you, what if making more good choices than bad ones was your only expectation? How would that change the way you feel?

Others' Expectations

An expectation is an agreement you make with yourself about what you will or will not do, but it often begins with an agreement others want you to make. Sometimes what others want isn't what you want, isn't what God wants for you, or simply isn't doable. And yet fear, especially fear of disapproval, can lead you to take on the burden of others' expectations as a way to avoid uncomfortable conversations or flat-out rejection.

When we don't take time to clarify our expectations of ourselves, we are typically left attempting to blindly meet everyone else's expectations. "Others" can be as close as your parents or children, or as distant as the vague "they" you can't even pinpoint but believe have opinions and expectations about how you should live your life. In today's world, "others" can also include the messages we consume from social media and traditional media, celebrities, and spiritual and political influencers.

Figuring out who you are and what you believe takes self-reflection and work. It's easier to let people tell you what your expectations ought to be, especially if embracing those expectations means approval and acceptance. Real growth happens when you question every expectation you have embraced and ask:

- *Is this my expectation or someone else's?*
- *If this is my expectation, why does it matter to me?*
- *If it isn't my expectation, where did it come from?*
- *What would be a wise expectation of me in this season of my life?*

What to Do Next

To reset the expectations that create false guilt for you, coach yourself through the process using the prompts I give you below. Resetting expectations is powerful, and it takes practice. Once you identify your new expectations, keep them in front of you. You may want to write them down, set a reminder on your phone, or share them with a friend who can help keep you reminded and accountable when the false guilt from old expectations starts to creep in.

Think about the guilt dilemmas that plague you most right now. Jot them down here:

_____

_____

_____

_____

At the core of false guilt is an expectation that needs to be reset.

I invite you right now to reset expectations that are causing you false guilt because you either cannot meet the expectation or because the expectation doesn't even line up with what you want and care about. Ask yourself:

- *What is my expectation here?*
- *Where did this expectation come from?*
- *Have I made this expectation specific enough to know when it has been met?*
- *Does this expectation reflect what's important to me?*

As you begin to see how expectations can be a setup for false guilt, go one step further to consider where those expectations come from.

It can be easy to insist that you only want your own acceptance and God's acceptance. But the truth of the matter is that that takes deep inner work. That takes a lot of trust. That takes not caring what others think—and regardless of how many times we might say we don't care what others think, it is easier said than done. And yet, it is necessary if we are to break the chains of bondage that perfectionism represents.

Consider the areas where you have expectations that fit into one of the categories I've described in this book: vague expectations, outdated expectations, unbalanced expectations, perfectionistic expectations, and others' expectations. What expectations do you currently attempt to meet that need to be reset? List them here.

_____

_____

_____

_____

Use these four steps to hit the reset button and create authentic expectations that you can meet with joy, peace, and ease.

GIVE YOUR INNER VOICE A NEW SCRIPT: Make sure your inner voice lets go of guilt rather than piling it on. You don't necessarily choose the thoughts that show up, but you do choose which ones you repeat. What are you saying to yourself when you beat yourself up for not meeting expectations? Replace those thoughts with ones that are more helpful. *I have permission to be imperfect. I choose joy over guilt. Feeling good is good. I choose to feel good. I forgive myself for falling short and thank God for the grace to learn from this.*

GIVE YOURSELF PERMISSION TO RESET EXPECTATIONS THAT CREATE GUILT: Only you can decide to reset expectations so you set yourself up for joy instead of guilt. Focus on thoughts such as *I have permission to reset the expectation in this situation. A wiser expectation would be . . .*

IDENTIFY THE NEW EXPECTATION: In the five categories of expectations, use the coaching questions that follow to identify a new expectation you'd like to replace your old expectation with.

VAGUE EXPECTATIONS: Get specific. What is a specific, measurable expectation that reflects what's most important to you, and what is a timeline for meeting that expectation?

OUTDATED EXPECTATIONS: Honor the new season you're in by setting expectations that make sense given your commitments, personal growth, and vision at this time. In what ways are your expectations outdated, and what should you take into consideration now that wasn't a factor before? In this season of your life, what do you want the expectation to be?

UNBALANCED EXPECTATIONS: Release the thought that you owe more than others in your relationships. Instead, embrace reciprocal relationships. In what way is there an unbalanced dynamic? Where are you being overresponsible? What would a balanced expectation look like?

PERFECTIONISTIC EXPECTATIONS: When do you tend to be defensive, make comparisons, or become especially harsh in your self-criticism? What expectations do you have of yourself that trigger those reactions? What new expectations could you set instead—expectations that would leave you feeling you've done enough?

OTHERS' EXPECTATIONS: Whose expectations do you most often feel guilty about not living up to? Are those expectations a reflection of your values and divine assignments? If not, what expectation can you drop or adjust? What will be the new expectation?

COMMUNICATE NEW EXPECTATIONS: If your new expectations involve others, or new boundaries you will have with them, have a conversation to communicate your new expectations. If the expectation is purely personal, make it visible. Put a note where you'll see it often (like on your desk, your mirror, or your dashboard) or set a reminder on your phone with an affirmation that pops up each day reminding you of your new expectation until it becomes your new normal.

Flip the Guilt Trip

Deactivate the Buttons Manipulators Like to Push

- Which buttons always get the same reaction from you?
- Is your tendency to feel false guilt attracting guilt trippers?
- What are nine signs you are being guilt-tripped?

"Why couldn't I be born into a family that could pay for college? I had to graduate with all this debt!" Jason said to his mom, Joy.

It wasn't the first time. "Jason is a button pusher," Joy said. "Sometime after puberty he started using guilt trips. It's as though he just wants me to feel I owe him something more. I have told him he is spoiled and unrealistic, but that doesn't change anything."

———

Amanda never feels guilt trips from her kids. When she hears the word *guilt*, she immediately thinks of her mother.

"I could never just have my mother over for conversation. Instead, it is always an evaluation. She sizes up my home, my parenting skills, my cooking, my husband, my weight, you name it!" she said with anxiety in her voice. "And she's not direct about it. Instead, she just starts asking questions: 'Have you noticed your carpet's getting worn out over here in the living room? Isn't it about time to start cooking dinner? It's four o'clock. When are you going to get Mikey into Pull-Ups? It's about time, isn't it?' Nothing I do is ever good enough, and it has always been this way."

Amanda said it's so bad that she hears her mother's voice in her head anytime she wants to take a break, sit down, and watch TV. "I can hear her saying, 'Why are you sitting? You should be doing laundry. You should be cooking. You're being lazy.' But if we are together in person, it is constant—questions about why I am not doing something more, expectations about what I should do for her.

"My mom has given me guilt my entire existence," she recalled. "Whatever I did, I was never doing enough."

But even worse, her mother expected Amanda would invite her to social outings with Amanda's friends or include her in activities that Amanda may have wanted to do alone with her children.

"If I don't invite my mom to every single thing I do, there's hell to pay," she said. "I can't host my girlfriends at my house or take my kids to a kids' movie without her, even though she'd complain because she doesn't even like kids' movies! If she finds out, she'll say, 'Well, you should have at least asked if I wanted to go.'"

Amanda said she got the silent treatment as punishment for

these incidents. "She won't talk to me for three days. She'll send a text instead of call on a birthday. It's really hurtful."

———

The guilt trips Ava dealt with came from her husband. "He pretty much invalidates any of my struggles by suggesting he's had it much worse," she said, frustrated. It put their marriage in a very precarious place. Ava found herself constantly adjusting her behavior to please him, but it was never enough. They got married planning to have children, but a couple of years in, he announced that he really didn't want kids and that he didn't think she was "organized enough" to be a mom.

"You wash clothes on different days of the week, we don't have dinner at the same time every night, and you've got a lot on your plate at work," he told her matter-of-factly. "I don't know how you think you can handle adding 'mom' to your to-do list."

As ridiculous as it sounds, Ava began doubting her basic organizational abilities. She responded to his criticisms by trying to create more of a predictable routine and reading articles about how to be more organized.

Then he threw new requirements at her. "I need you to explain why you want to be a mom," he told her. And when she said, "I just always imagined myself with children. I love children. I want to have a family," he said her answer didn't have purpose and she needed a better reason for bringing children into the world. Anytime the topic would come up, Ava ended up feeling as though she was somehow wrong for wanting children. She began to question whether she should have children.

"I literally began to feel guilty for wanting to be a mother," she remembered. "We'd go for months and even up to a year at a time without talking about it because the conversation would always lead to something I wasn't doing to deserve to have a family."

Guilt Trips

A guilt trip is a manipulative way of getting someone to do something they wouldn't otherwise do by causing them to feel guilty. The feeling of debt brought on by the guilt then sways the person's behavior and decisions in a way that benefits the guilt tripper. False guilt is basically a guilt trip you take yourself on. But the guilt trips others attempt to drag us on can be harder to overcome. This type of guilt trip is about making someone feel guilty, especially in order to induce them to do something.

Here are a few signs you are being guilt-tripped. Think about someone who tries to influence you through guilt. How many of these nine signs are present in your relationships?

1. **YOU NEVER SEEM TO BE ABLE TO MEET THE OTHER PERSON'S EXPECTATIONS.** It feels like you are always doing something wrong. You don't meet the other person's standards. In essence, nothing you do is good enough.
2. **THE OTHER PERSON COMPARES YOU TO PEOPLE WHO ARE SOMEHOW DOING BETTER THAN YOU.** You are compared to others who meet expectations as proof that you are in the wrong and need to change.

3. **THE OTHER PERSON CAN'T MAKE IT WITHOUT YOU.** Even though the guilt tripper isn't pleased with you, they will insist they need you. They will make sure you know you have put them in an awful predicament because you have now made them vulnerable by not living up to their expectations. So you are stuck in a place of doing them harm if you don't figure out how to live up to their expectations. The other person doesn't want you to walk away; they just want you to step in line and do what they want.

4. **YOU OVER-THANK AND OVER-COMPLIMENT THE OTHER PERSON.** Remember, guilt means you owe, so when you feel guilt-tripped, you will feel you owe that person a debt of gratitude—after all, they are putting up with you and all the stuff you're not doing right. Because you feel unworthy or devalued, you may overvalue the other person and overestimate the worth of their contributions compared to yours.

5. **THE OTHER PERSON QUESTIONS YOUR LOVE OR LOYALTY.** If you hear, "If you loved me, you would . . ." or "If you cared about this the way I do, you would . . ." you are being guilt-tripped. This tactic tempts you to prove them wrong, which gets you to do whatever they said you would do if only you cared about them or the situation at hand.

6. **YOU FEEL LIKE YOU CAN'T SAY NO WITHOUT SEVERE CONSEQUENCES.** You feel obligated. You owe; therefore, you can't say no. The consequences are just not worth it, so you bow to the pressure just to keep the peace. You're not happy, but the alternative feels worse.

7. **YOU'RE ALWAYS THE ONE TO BLAME WHEN SOME-THING GOES WRONG.** You are the one who needs to be guided, taught, and corrected. That's because everything is your fault—even, or perhaps especially, when it's not. Guilt trippers rarely own up to their part in problems. Any guilt they feel they project on to you or some other unfortunate soul.

8. **THEY ARE SACRIFICING TO BE IN RELATIONSHIP WITH YOU.** The relationship feels out of balance—because it is. It is like a debtor-lender relationship: they've done you a favor or "endured" your failing their standards, so they are the sacrificial lamb, putting up with you. You ought to just be grateful they are so good at living up to their high standards and duties to be your friend, coworker, significant other, etc.

9. **YOU WORK HARD TO MEET THEIR EXPECTATIONS, BUT THEY DON'T EVEN KNOW WHAT YOUR EXPECTATIONS ARE!** Guilt trippers are good at setting expectations. They do it early and often, sometimes before you've even thought about yours. So their expectations become the standard. And those expectations are advantageous to them. Your expectations, if you have any, might rarely even make it into the conversation.

I like Urban Dictionary's straight-to-the-point definition of guilt trip: "A manipulation tactic: making someone feel guilty so that guilt acts as an incentive to think or behave a way they normally wouldn't. Often involves the manipulator acting victimized or making grand gestures to create emotional debt."[1]

Why We Go Along with Guilt Trips

No one can force you onto a guilt trip. You have to willingly go for the ride. Why, then, is it so easy to end up there? Here are a few reasons:

- **IT COMES FROM SOMEONE YOU CARE ABOUT.** Guilt trips only work with people close to you. If there's no real emotional connection, guilt trips don't work.
- **YOU FEAR THE REPERCUSSIONS.** Guilt trippers typically dangle a threat before you. It isn't always a blatant demand; sometimes it's implied. Nonetheless, you can rest assured there'll be consequences if you don't go along with it. Whether it's the silent treatment or disapproval or something more tangible, you fear the repercussions.
- **YOU ACTUALLY AGREE WITH THE ACCUSATION.** On some level, the guilt trip works because you buy into the belief that the accusation is true. This is why it is critical to examine your thoughts—especially when those thoughts are seeds planted by a guilt tripper.

Erin is kind, pretty, smart, hardworking, and riddled with guilt. When asked what makes her feel guilty, her response was, "Everything."

Her biggest culprit was the guilt trips she said her mother had always laid on her. "I just feel like I am not a good enough daughter to my mom," she said with a tinge of anxiety in her voice. "No matter what I do for her, it's not enough. It's like a hole that can never be filled, and yet I keep trying to fill it—to no avail!"

Recently Erin took her mom on a trip to visit cousins in

Denver. They went sightseeing at Pike's Peak, spent a day in the mountains, and even had a little birthday celebration since her mom's birthday fell during the trip. Erin and one of her cousins bought a cake, they brought gifts, they sang "Happy Birthday." It was a lovely trip—and that's saying a lot, according to Erin, because typically her mother finds something to complain about. This time, she didn't.

Then they got back home, and a few days later someone in the family mentioned celebrating her mom's birthday. Her mom's response? "Yeah, I didn't get a birthday celebration this year."

Erin was stunned. "Mom, what do you mean? We celebrated your birthday in Denver, remember? I bought you a cake. We sang 'Happy Birthday.' You opened gifts."

"Well, that doesn't count," she told Erin. "You didn't plan that. Your cousin did." Never mind the celebration was Erin's idea and she made it all happen with the help of her cousin. Apparently it wasn't enough.

Guilt trips are rooted in the idea that you owe. The person laying the guilt trip on you is adept at finding ways to tip the relationship out of balance so you feel you have not done enough or they have done more than their share. They put guilt in the driver's seat of your relationship in order to take it in the direction they'd like it to go. All they need is for you to go along for the ride.

Guilt trippers are master manipulators. They will often say little things to plant the seeds of guilt, hoping you'll respond by doing what they want or "pay" by feeling badly about something. The purpose of the guilt trip is to influence your actions and decisions. Remember that it is not enough to become aware of what triggers your guilt. You must also take charge of the fight-or-flight reaction that guilt can trigger. Guilt trippers may not know what goes on in your brain when guilt is induced, but they do know how powerful it can be as an influencer of behavior. If they can get inside your head and create feelings of guilt, there is a chance your fight-or-flight reaction will be as swift as if a bear were running after you.

The thing is, though, a guilt trip is not a demand. It is an invitation you have the right to decline. Though there may be threats and conquences, you ultimately have a choice to deal with the consequnces rather than allowing yourself to be manipulated.

> Guilt trippers may not know what goes on in your brain when guilt is induced, but they do know how powerful it can be as an influencer of behavior.

An extreme example of this is Edye Frankel, one of the youngest survivors of the Holocaust. Edye is the mother of one of my dear friends, and when I mentioned during a family gathering at my friend's house that I was writing this book, Edye quickly chimed in about her own struggle with guilt. I was intrigued as she described feeling guilty about not remembering her time in three separate concentration camps as a baby and toddler, feeling her lack of memory somehow diminished her right to call herself a survivor. I asked her if I could interview her about her experiences at they related to guilt. During our interview a few months later, she shared how an expectation planted by her rabbi in her twenties led to deep guilt. Edye's story is worthy of an entire book, but I'm going to share just this small piece of it as an example of how others' expectations can take us on a guilt trip.

In her twenties, Edye fell in love and got engaged to be

married. There was just one major problem, in her father's eyes anyway. Her fiancé was not Jewish. "My husband was black," she explained. "That was beside the point. If he had converted, my father would have reluctantly accepted him." Her husband did not convert, and Edye did not back down in the face of her father's threats that she marry someone Jewish or be disowned.

After she married, her father followed through on his threat. She was twenty-two. "He mourned my death," she said. "He destroyed my birth certificate. He died before we ever talked again." It was a courageous choice not to go along with his guilt trip. She paid a tremendous price.

While his attempt to control Edye's choice of marriage partner via threats could have been a deep source of guilt for Edye, she said her decision to marry someone her father did not approve of was not a lingering source of guilt.

"I was very stubborn," she said. "You've got to be true to yourself. I followed my own principles in whatever I did."

However, to this day Edye still experiences guilt from a conversation with her rabbi in the midst of the conflict with her father. "I promised the rabbi that I would raise my children Jewish," she reflected. "That's why I felt guilty. It was deeper. The Holocaust happened to us because we're Jewish. To give up the religion would be to give up the reason we endured so much."

The rabbi impressed upon Edye that it was her responsibility to her faith and to her people to make sure her children were raised Jewish. "Anytime someone leaves the religion it reduces the population," she said she was told.

So she enrolled them in Hebrew school at the synagogue. "The other children made fun of them," she said. "They called them names. They were very cruel."

Soon, she put them in public school where their friends were mostly black. At the Jewish school, they were criticized for not being "Jewish enough." At the public school, they weren't "black enough." Edye did her best to help them navigate their world, and as much as she wanted their race and religion not to matter, the world they entered each day insisted it did. When her oldest asked, "What color am I, Mommy?" she told her, "You're people color." But the neighborhood kids rejected that idea. Exasperated, she said, "Society says you have to be black, so that's what it's going to be."

Edye's strong sense of fairness and justice, born of her experience of prejudice while growing up and as a survivor of the Holocaust, led her to teach her daughters that all religions are good. "I had seders at my house with all sorts of people of different religions and races, and it was wonderful." Ultimately, her daughters did not maintain their Jewish faith, and Edye blamed herself. "I cried for days when I got the news that one of my daughters would be baptized," she admits. "It was so painful to me. It took resolve to get over it. I let time pass. I just made a value judgment. How important is religion versus my own children?"

It is a rather ironic question given that her father chose religion over his daughter. Even more ironic is Edye's reflection that perhaps the personal trials that resulted from her first marriage were of her own making, because of guilt. "I created situations for myself to cause pain so I would create my own Holocaust," she said, hypothesizing that perhaps her inability to remember the Holocaust triggered decisions to create painful situations.

The guilt Edye felt for not succeeding in meeting the rabbi's request was deep, and it was more extreme than most of us will ever experience when it comes to guilt, but it illustrates just how powerful guilt trips are. She maintained her values around racial and religious equality when she married against her father's wishes. But the expectation of raising her children in the faith was one that, ultimately, was not her choice to make. It was an expectation beyond her control.

"It's hard to say what I should have done differently. I didn't want to shove anything down their throats. I didn't want to force them to do anything. It was a feeling of fairness," she said. Perhaps her value of fairness was incongruent with the expectation of her rabbi's request. The two values collided. Guilt was inevitable.

While it may not appear on the surface to be a guilt trip, implicit in both her father's demands and her rabbi's request was the idea that she owed. She owed it to her people and to those who'd suffered to carry on her faith and her heritage. Ultimately, though, Edye allowed her values around fairness and love to guide her decisions. And that meant her own children could make decisions free of the threats and expectations she had once faced.

Guilt Attracts Guilt Trippers

Erin, the woman who had been struggling with guilt trips from her mother, shared an interesting tidbit. For more than a decade, beginning in high school, her best friend used guilt trips to control who else she was friends with. "I feel like I am a magnet for this kind of thing," she said.

It's a terrible thought, but there just may be some truth to the idea that when we carry false guilt, we attract people who pounce on our vulnerability. Just think about it: if you use guilt trips to get what you want, you lose control when you engage in relationships with people who won't take the bait. Instead, like any other abuser, you seek out people who will go along with your manipulation and emotional abuse.

Craig is, unfortunately, a perfect example. He said he was a quintessential nice kid in his teenage years. He was kind, funny, easy to be around. He was also privileged in some ways. His family was fairly well-off, and he never thought much about money because he never had to. But his parents often requested that he and his siblings play down their lifestyle when visiting family.

"They didn't want anyone in the family to feel like we had more than they did. I wasn't allowed to even talk about my achievements in school," he remembered. "I think I started to catch on that maybe our blessings were something others would be offended by or jealous of."

As he got older, a pattern began to emerge in his friendships. "It seemed like I gravitated toward people who didn't have as much. I don't remember doing it consciously, but looking back, it happened throughout my teen years and twenties." Craig said he had friends who made comments implying he didn't deserve what he had, and that if he was a real friend, he'd give them money.

"The guilt trip that was hung over my head was that I thought I was better than other people and that I didn't deserve the blessings I had," he explained. "And it was true that I didn't deserve the blessings. I mean, it's not like I picked my family. I lucked out being born into my family. But it was not true that I thought I was better than others." That accusation really bothered Craig, and looking back, he realizes it was a guilt trip that worked.

"I was often manipulated into buying things for people, fixing problems when they were irresponsible. As crazy as it sounds, I stayed in a relationship much too long in my twenties, in part because I was trying to prove I didn't think I was better than people in a different economic bracket. There was a constant refrain in our relationship that my life was easier than hers and I should feel guilty and pay for that. I don't even want to begin to think about all the ways I paid—helping out her and her family, buying gifts, and meeting other expectations that began to spiral out of control."

Craig finally began to see how he had been manipulated by people who saw his guilt-prone thinking as a vulnerability they could take advantage of. He began to choose his friendships and relationships differently and set boundaries with those who tended to be manipulative. As he did, he says the guilt trippers sought out his friendship less and less.

Manipulative people want to push your buttons and get a predictable reaction from you. Guilt is a tool for them. When you deactivate those buttons, the tool is no longer useful. They'll push from new angles to see if they can reactivate the old guilt buttons, but if you remain steady, they'll soon give up and move to someone who is easier to manipulate.

Self-Induced Guilt Trips

Some guilt trips are not as obvious. These are the guilt trips that go on almost entirely in your head as you imagine that someone will be upset, that you will be seen as selfish, or that others deserve more than you.

Claire was a master at the self-induced guilt trip, and she didn't even realize it. Smart, sweet, and hardworking, she wanted coaching on how to get over some of her social anxieties, but she had never connected the idea of guilt with her anxiety. Her deepest desire was to feel seen and valued, something she was good at doing for others. But she often feared others' criticism and felt overlooked.

Claire shared something curious with me during a coaching session. A high achiever in a *Fortune* 500 company, she had once received an internal award for her efforts on behalf of the company. It was a big deal, and she had earned it. Her parents always sent her flowers when good things happened, and on this particular day when they called to chat and tell her how proud they were, she made a request.

"Please don't send me flowers this time," she said.

"But why? It is such a wonderful accomplishment! This is our way of celebrating how special you are."

She hesitated before answering. "I don't want to make other people feel bad," she said. "It'll just cause problems."

I was floored. Claire had pushed away the very thing she said she wanted—a gesture of feeling seen and valued. It was a theme for her. She often downplayed her accomplishments. She said it was because she didn't want others to be uncomfortable, but now that she had made a career transition out of corporate America to lead her own digital marketing firm, she often found herself in a setting where she needed to introduce herself to new people. These people had no idea of her background, and because she downplayed her accomplishments, their perceptions of who she is and what she is capable of fell far below reality. It was impacting her ability to win new business.

"Why do you hide who you really are?" I asked. "What makes you want to shrink so that other people feel comfortable?"

"Because there are repercussions when people are uncomfortable with you," she said.

Claire's guilt trip stemmed from a handful of people who had criticized her in the past, and she allowed the guilt trips they laid on her to play over and over again in her mind. These old guilt trips continued to work in new environments and situations.

This is her guilty statement: *It is wrong to celebrate your hard work and achievements because it might make someone else feel they haven't done enough.*

If you look a little deeper, though, you'll notice something more about what is driving her guilt—self-preservation. The thought is this: *If others are uncomfortable, there will be a price to pay.* Remember that when you peel back the layers on guilt, you'll sometimes find that guilt is not about what it at first appears to be. Self-induced guilt trips are often about protecting oneself from the wrath of others.

In Claire's case, she decided to peel back one more layer to ask a critical, powerful question. "What if others are uncomfortable? What then?" In other words, rather than allowing fear to tell her that there would be a price to pay, she asked a question that would force her to decide whether it was a price worth paying.

Someone else's discomfort is not your problem to solve when solving it means diminishing your purpose and work. You don't need to be rude about it, but you must stand fully in who you are regardless of what others may think. Those who use guilt trips want to control you by heaping false guilt on you. But you don't have to take the bait. You will, however, have to get comfortable with being uncomfortable at times. You will have to examine your thoughts and decide whether they are true or false, and replace the false ones with truth. By learning to let go, you deactivate the buttons manipulators like to push to get you to do what they want.

Reciprocity and Guilt

My son Alex came running from his golf camp with a little piece of paper in his hand. He was beaming with the sort of excitement only a five-year-old can conjure up over a fast-food coupon. Granted, it was a Chick-fil-A coupon, so I get it. "Mommy, we can go buy a free kid's meal with this!" he exclaimed.

We stopped at Chick-fil-A on the way home. It was only 11:00 a.m., and I wasn't hungry. There was some delicious chicken in the fridge that my husband had grilled the night before. I planned to eat that for lunch around 1:00.

We pulled into a parking space right in front of the door. Alex was still excited as we walked up to the Chick-fil-A counter to place his order. "Hi," I said to the guy behind the counter with his freshly pressed polo shirt. "I have this coupon for a kid's meal, so we'll have a chicken nugget kid's meal with a chocolate milk." That was the end of the order I had planned. That was all I came for.

But I felt a little knot in my stomach. I think it was brought on by some thoughts that went something like this: *So you're going to come in here with your free coupon, order only the free food, use the restroom, let your son play on the playground while you clear out some e-mails, and then leave without spending a dime?*

My answer to that question should have been simply, *Yes. Yes, that's exactly what I'm about to do.* But you know the guilt drill. Guilt answered the question loud and clear: *That is just rude. You don't go into a restaurant, get free food, use the facilities, and not order anything!*

The next thing out of my mouth was, ". . . And I'll have a Chick-fil-A sandwich, no pickle, a fruit cup, and a bottle of water, please." I wasn't hungry. I had lunch waiting for me at home. Shoot, I wasn't even thirsty! But I ordered out of guilt.

There's a name for this. Robert Cialdini, author of *Influence* and professor at Arizona State University, talks about the power of reciprocity in marketing. Essentially, when we're given something as a gift, even if it is something we don't value, we feel obligated in some way to the giver.[2] It's the reason a nonprofit will send you free address labels you didn't ask for. It's a clever use of the guilt trip as a marketing strategy. They know that a large enough percentage of recipients will feel guilty about not paying for the free gift. Remember, one of the three truths of guilt is that guilt is a debt; it says you owe. So a free coupon can create guilt if you let it—that is, if you don't label the emotion and pause before reacting to it.

Guilty People Guilt People

Most of us have heard the saying "hurting people hurt people," meaning that those who have been hurt make decisions out of their pain and hurt others in the process. There is a similar phenomenon when it comes to guilt. Those who feel guilty and have not worked through their guilt often cope by laying that guilt on other people. Beware.

One of the most devastating examples I encountered was a fellow speaker who talked about how her journey of love and motherhood was impacted by a woman in her church who pulled her aside to discourage her from adopting a child. She was over forty at the time and single. The woman didn't discourage her because it might be difficult to raise a child alone. Instead, the woman used a deep wound she'd worked hard to overcome as a weapon against her. She'd been molested as a child. The woman said to her, "If you were molested, you really shouldn't have children." The implication was that the damage done in her devastating childhood somehow should disqualify her from motherhood. This twisted advice came from a woman who herself was riddled with guilt about her own past. The advice did not come from a place of wisdom or love or truth, but instead from a place of guilt, shame, and pain. Nonetheless, she took the advice—the expectation—of a guilty, toxic person. She had been on the verge of adopting and abandoned the idea entirely. She gave up on her dream. Years passed before she peeled back the layers and created new expectations, rooted in truth, and at age fifty adopted a child.

Have the Hard Conversation

If you are being guilt tripped, you may need to have a hard conversation in order to break free. So let's break down what it takes to have a hard conversation effectively. If you've been operating in guilt and the people close to you are used to it, they will likely resist some of what you have to say. Do not let this deter you. Every once in a while, they'll be totally honest and recognize that the conversation is overdue. They'll acknowledge that change is needed and you are being reasonable. That happens when someone is emotionally available and able to have uncomfortable conversations. But when that's not the case, make the decision to have the hard conversation anyway. Be the bigger person. Be brave.

Fear often comes from focusing on what might go wrong rather than focusing on what could go right. When we step out of our comfort zones, we can catastrophize about the direction a hard conversation is going to take. We play an entire movie in our heads about the negative consequences of telling the truth, of asking for what you need and want, and hurting someone's feelings. But it is just as important to focus on what could go right. In other words, when you need to have a hard conversation, you must bring the skill of thought awareness to bear. Rather than shutting thoughts down, explore them. Acknowledge them. And then make a strategy to move forward despite them.

Think about the hard conversation it's time for you to have in order to set a boundary or a new expectation. Then ask yourself these questions:

- *What am I afraid will happen if I have this conversation?*
- *How would I handle it if that happened?*
- *What are all the benefits of me having this conversation?*
- *What do I want to happen as a result of this conversation?*
- *What specifically do I need to say?*
- *What am I most afraid of saying, and why?*
- *What if I begin by describing my fear and anxiety and then explain that despite my fear and anxiety, I am having this conversation because it's so important?*

By honestly revealing that you have anxiety, you communicate to the other person the importance of the conversation. You communicate your concern. You communicate that you care about them and you don't want to damage the relationship, but that you also feel called to tell the truth and to do what God is leading you to do.

Your Script to Abandon a Guilt Trip

In the rest of the chapter, I've laid out six steps that will lead you out of a guilt trip and onto a path of truth and freedom. With each step, I'm giving you the exact words you can use or tweak in a conversation with the guilt tripper.

Deactivate the guilt-trip button.

Guilt trips work because people have learned how to get you to react to a guilt trigger. They activate the trigger, and you do what they want. This occurs because you react rather than respond. Responding means you pause and consciously choose what action you will or won't take. So the first way to deactivate the button is to not do what you would normally do. If you usually comply, don't. If you normally start apologizing profusely for things you didn't actually do wrong, stop. If you open up your wallet and start doling out cash, keep your wallet closed.

SCRIPT

Say nothing. Do not react right away.

Or say, "I'm not going to be able to do that."

Or, "I'll think about it and let you know."

Then say nothing else. No explanation. When you begin trying to explain, especially while you are learning this new way of responding, you can accidentally talk your way back into the guilt trip!

Label the guilt.

Remember that naming the emotion helps you consciously notice it as it rises within you, allowing you to pause. Guilt trips trigger a fight-or-flight reaction. Labeling the guilt slows down this process. Labeling simply means that you make a mental note that guilt has shown up and just might try to get in the driver's seat.

SCRIPT

Say to yourself: "I am feeling guilty. What's that all about?"

If you are unsure of whether it is false guilt or authentic guilt, use the PEEL process to get your answer.

Call out the guilt.

Guilt thrives in the dark. Guilt trippers and manipulators count on you to quietly comply. They know you are uncomfortable with confrontation, so they will use that fear to control the situation. Remember, guilt is sneaky, so call it out. This works whether it is a self-induced guilt trip or a guilt trip from someone else. Be honest with yourself so you can be honest with others.

SCRIPT

Say this to the guilt tripper: "I don't like to do things out of guilt because it makes me feel resentful. I like to do things because I feel led to do it and I know it is what I am supposed to do."

Request the guilt tripper make a request.

Those who use guilt trips are often just as uncomfortable with having honest conversations and confrontation. That's why they are not direct. Their passive-aggressive approach allows them to get what they want without discomfort. Making you uncomfortable is their comfort zone. So it's up to you to take the conversation and relationship outside your norm.

SCRIPT

Tell your guilt tripper: "I know there is something specific you'd like from me, and I'm asking you to make a request without the guilt trip."

Ask the guilt tripper to respect your decisions.

Acknowledge that you understand what the guilt tripper wants is important to them, but you must make decisions that are wise and make sense for you. Ask them to respect your decision. That means that once you've made the decision, they let it go, accept it, and make alternative plans that respect your choice, rather than gossiping or badmouthing you or going behind your back to get others to influence you to change your mind.

SCRIPT

Tell your guilt tripper: "I understand you think I should do something else, but this is the decision that makes sense for me. I am asking you to respect my right to make my decision."

Affirm the person's value in your life.

Like I've said, guilt trips tend to work best when it is someone close to you, someone whose opinion and good graces matter to you. So tell them that.

SCRIPT

Let your guilt tripper know: "I care what you think."

"I don't like being in conflict with you."

"I don't enjoy letting you down."

"I want to meet your expectation, but I can't."

Expect to repeat the discussion until habits change.

I know you want the guilt trips to stop—today. But since you cannot control others' behavior, know that it may take them a minute to catch on to your new thought patterns and boundaries. Hold firm, though. Have the conversation more than once if needed. Keep calling out the guilt trip. Shine a light on it. Request they be direct. Implement consequences if they don't stop. For example, a consequence could be as minor as walking out of the room when they don't honor your request or as significant as ending a friendship if they refuse to stop. Think ahead of time about what the consequences will be and be prepared to carry them out. You can communicate the consequences in a direct but kind tone. It may feel uncomfortable, but it is also freeing to set boundaries in a such a clear way.

The dynamic of the relationship may have developed over time. If it is ingrained, you'll need to continue this new style of communication until it becomes ingrained instead.

SCRIPT

Say to your guilt tripper: "As we talked about before . . . [describe what your previous request was]. It is important that you stop because the guilt trips are damaging our relationship by creating resentment, and I don't want to feel that toward you."

Practice love and patience.

First Corinthians 13:5 says love keeps no record of wrongs. Regardless of whether the guilt tripper shows love, you can choose how you want to behave. Remember that guilt trips are about control. If they can get you to react in ways that make you guilty of something, they will use it against you. Again, don't take the bait. You can sabotage your best efforts at setting a boundary by flying off the handle or dishonoring someone, especially someone close to you. Be the bigger person. Be truthful, yet kind. Be direct, yet gentle.

What to Do Next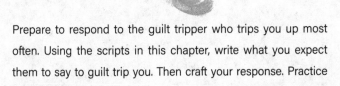

Prepare to respond to the guilt tripper who trips you up most often. Using the scripts in this chapter, write what you expect them to say to guilt trip you. Then craft your response. Practice it out loud.

NINE

Take Back Your Joy

Embrace the Eight Habits of Guilt-Free Living

- What would joy look like for you?
- What are signs you are guilt-free?
- How can you use happiness triggers to boost your joy?

A powerful milestone in the journey to let go of the guilt occurs when you no longer have to focus on "letting go" because you never grabbed hold of guilt in the first place. It is a sign that you've untangled guilt's grip. Guilt might show up at the doorstep of your mind, but there's no open door for it to come in.

Arriving at this milestone signals the point in your journey where the focus of your energy is on what you want rather than what you don't. A powerful goal can never simply be the absence of something. It must be a declaration of the presence of something. It's not enough to let go of your guilt. Letting it go will certainly feel better than wallowing in it, but at some point you'll realize "letting go" is not your deepest desire. Your spirit longs for something more. Your spirit desires joy. It desires peace. It desires love.

In my case, my spirit wanted freedom to make decisions that represented my authentic values and desires. I wanted the freedom to move toward the life I believe God has in store. For me, that meant caring more about God's expectations for me than others' expectations, especially since some of the "others" were only in my head. It meant I might disappoint some people. It meant I might have to let go of unrealistic expectations I had of myself and others—mourning the loss of an illusion of what life ought to look like and accepting the reality of what it could be right now.

Acceptance Clears the Path for Joy

I knew I had made real progress on my journey to let go of the guilt and embrace joy the day I recorded this simple experience in my journal.

What is this feeling I have right now, when I would normally feel guilt? I got up before 5:00 a.m. and didn't write anywhere near my goal. It feels like a resignation to my own lack of productivity. It is an acceptance, rather than guilt. I'm not giving up, so what's the point of feeling guilty? What if this is just part of the process, and rather than being shocked by it, I accept it and simply continue moving forward toward the finish line? No wasted energy, no beating myself up for not getting more done. Just pure acceptance of my imperfection in my own ridiculous, slow, overthinking process, which I have repeated multiple times to satisfying success.

Acceptance is your ability to see the truth and have the courage to act on it. It is to see that your guilt is false and stop making decisions based on that false guilt. It is to see when you are wrong and walk through the process of admitting guilt, apologizing, and atoning for it. It is to label the guilt trip a guilt trip and refuse to go along for the ride. But acceptance takes practice. And the more you do it, the freer you feel as you clear the path for joy in your life in places where there has been none. Whenever you feel yourself resisting acceptance, say to yourself, *I see the truth, and I choose to respond with love and courage.*

The opposite of acceptance is resistance. To release guilt, we must notice what we are resisting. Resistance represents our blocks to joy, peace, love, and truth. It often shows up as fear. What does it look like to "resist" rather than accept? We resist reality by avoiding honest, tough conversations, pretending the truth isn't the truth, and suppressing our values and needs in order to meet others' expectations. When we accept what is, good or bad, we can do the work we must do to let go of our guilt. We can look honestly at self-sabotaging thoughts and replace them with truth. And by doing so, we make space for a life that is emotionally honest and peaceful, a space where joy abounds.

Acceptance is a bridge from guilt to freedom. On the other side of that bridge, you are free to have more authentic relationships, forgive yourself for your mistakes and regrets, receive God's forgiveness and love for you, and embrace the unique purpose for your life, which may look quite different from those around you.

One of the most important concepts we must embrace is the

acceptance of our own uniqueness. You are not here by accident. God created you for a purpose, and there are unique, divine assignments for you. There are seasons of your life when you must tune in, understand your assignment, and make sure you are positioned well for your assignment. That often means your life doesn't look like the lives of those around you. The expectations you need to live up to may be completely different from others'. Accept that. Embrace it. Doing so frees you to have joy and confidence in your decisions and choices. It releases you from the bondage of guilt for expectations you were never meant to meet. Remember these two truths:

- Until you accept and embrace the unique life God created you for, you'll feel guilty for not living the life you think others expect of you.
- You cannot accept and embrace the unique life God created you for if you don't truly believe God created you for a purpose—a purpose that may look different from those around you.

Eight Habits to Take Back Your Joy

Just as guilt has been a habit, joy can become a habit—if you practice and make intentional choices. I've identified eight powerful practices for taking back your joy.

1. Notice that your joy is missing.

I was at my airport gate headed to a speaking engagement when a young woman came running up to me with my driver's license. I was perplexed at first, wondering who she was and why she had such an important possession of mine. Then she quickly explained that she'd found it on the floor in the terminal and scanned several gates looking for a passenger who matched my photo. It would have been a real headache if she'd not found me. I was going to be flying back home the very next day

> Until you accept and embrace the unique life God created you for, you'll feel guilty for not living the life you think others expect of you.

and wouldn't have been able to get through security without my ID. Since I'd already passed through security on this trip, I probably wouldn't have realized it was gone until I needed it the next day.

You won't go looking for what you never noticed was lost. Guilt can leave you in such a fog, feeling anxious and unhappy as you ruminate on what you think you've done wrong, that it doesn't really occur to you what's been taken from you. You can come to believe the goal is to get rid of the guilty feelings. But I believe God's desire for you is so much bigger than that. His plan is an abundant life, a life of peace and joy and freedom. He can restore your soul to its original, joyful state. You can get serious about allowing your soul to be restored, reclaim the joy that's buried there, and hold on to it. The first step is simply to notice your joy is gone when guilt is present.

Even if you can't remember the last time you felt peace and joy, the joy is there. It is your natural state. Look at small children with no cares in the world, before guilt or pressures or pain become a part of their reality. It's there. Do you want it back? Answering yes is the first step.

2. Accept the past.

There may be events in your past that you wish didn't exist, or conversations you wish you could go back and have over again so you could say things differently. There may be choices you'd *un*make—or make. But you can't. The past simply is; it won't change, and no amount of wishing will change that fact. Those who have the most joy know this and accept it.

To accept is to make peace. But acceptance can also bump up against your perceptions of yourself and who you want to be in the world. It can bump up against what we wish our lives were. You know, that ideal you have of yourself and your circumstances? If an event from the past doesn't line up with that ideal, we can cope by resisting the truth. By ignoring it. By rejecting the part of our story that doesn't line up with the dream of who we wish we were and how we wish things had been. And sometimes, acceptance means owning your values without apology. It is difficult to accept the past when you haven't made peace with what really matters to you.

This was my struggle. A part of me held up the stay-at-home mom as the ideal. I pictured my own mom at home with me. She spoke often, as I was growing up, about the joy of her time with me as a baby, how it felt like she had the perfect baby doll, only I was real. She spoke often of teaching me to read and write at a very young age. She never held up staying at home as some sort of ideal to aspire to, yet I internalized and even idealized it that way. The truth is, she was twenty years old when I was born. She had not yet begun a career or even college. She went to work part time by the time I was three. I went to nursery school. And by the time I was seven, she was in a full-time professional career. She finished college when I was thirteen. And by the time my much younger brother came along, staying at home wasn't an option.

When I decided to take back my joy, I had to look at my mom guilt, notice how it stole my joy, and decide to take it back. That required peeling back some layers to see where my guilt-inducing thoughts were coming from, and deciding specifically whether the way I was living my life somehow did not align with my values. I discovered that comparison was sabotaging my ability to accept my past—and my present circumstances. Comparing my life at forty to my mom's life at twenty set me up for guilt. And it diminished the uniqueness of my journey. I had to make a choice to own my life and choices. And if I couldn't do that, then I'd need to clarify my values and make some changes.

As I prayed for an answer, a truth rose in my spirit: my life was the way it was supposed to be. It was also the way I *wanted* it to be. At twenty, I didn't want to be married and raising a child. At forty, I did. My life was different from my mother's—and my life was also good. The only thing missing was my acceptance of it. With that acceptance came relief. Confidence. Peace. *Joy.*

Acceptance requires surrender—surrender to God's plan for your life and all that that plan entails. That includes the lessons we need to learn and the people who are conduits for us to learn them. All things can work together for good for those who love God and are called according to His purpose (Romans 8:28). What the Enemy means for evil (even guilt), God can somehow use for good (Genesis 50:20). If we believe these truths, we must live them.

Every woman whose story I shared in this book, who was willing to be coached using the tools I've shared, eventually said that acceptance was how they finally found peace and joy.

Monica, who felt guilt about the life she wasn't able to give the daughter she had at eighteen compared to her younger daughter, finally accepted the reality of that comparison. "You know, given the circumstances, it is amazing how strong and determined I was at that young age to give my daughter the best life I could," she reflected after her coaching. "No, it wasn't the ideal of what I wish I could have done for her. But it is absolutely the best I could have done with the resources and circumstances I had at that time."

3. Embrace humility.

It might seem counterintuitive to say that those who want to let go of guilt and embrace joy need to tap into humility to do so. After all, guilt says that you are concerned about others and not so arrogant that you don't feel the need to apologize, right? Well, yes and no. Guilt requires empathy, and it is other-focused. But embracing joy requires forgiveness of oneself. And before we can talk about you forgiving yourself, we must first talk about how hard it can be to see ourselves as imperfect. After all, you typically beat yourself up because you are angry with yourself for not being perfect enough to meet your own high expectations. It takes a certain confidence in your abilities to believe you can live up to those expectations in the first place. Accepting that you've fallen short without beating yourself up means accepting your own humanity.

When I was in my early twenties, I volunteered in a ministry at my church called the Decision Counseling Ministry. We learned the Romans Road, a sequence of scriptures that help a person to understand the purpose of Jesus' very existence and the path to following Him. There was a key scripture that was simple but profound and freeing: "For all have sinned and fall short of the glory of God" (Romans 3:23). None of us is perfect—period. The sooner we accept that we fall short, the easier it is to accept the imperfections of our past.

As I was doing interviews for this book, I asked my own mother if she'd share her perspective and experience with guilt. She told me she didn't feel any guilt. I was perplexed. I thought she did. There were times in my adulthood, particularly as my younger brother was growing up, that she wrote me to apologize for not being there more when I was a teenager. My parents separated when I was thirteen, and for two years I lived with my father in Colorado while my mother lived about a hundred miles away in Wyoming. Then when she moved back, I lived with her, but she worked two jobs. That meant she missed opportunities to be active in some of the things going on in my life. And although we weren't poor by any stretch, money was tight. But circumstances were different twenty years later, and as milestones occurred in my younger brother's teenage years, it began to really dawn on her just how many moments and opportunities she'd missed with me that she now had with him.

After the second or third apology years ago, I assured her I'd fully accepted her apology. I wasn't comparing. I had accepted the circumstances and difficulties of my teenage years in my family. I truly believe she'd done what she thought was best for me then, working hard to try to maintain the lifestyle we'd had before the separation. If she could do it over, she would make different choices. With twenty years of experience comes a lot more wisdom about what really matters in life. And that wisdom is not lost on me as I make choices with my own children.

I had assumed that she was beating herself up until I asked to talk to her about her guilt, and she responded that she didn't have any. I thought at first that maybe she was kidding herself, until she explained. "I accept all the choices I've made in my life and how it has turned out," she said with assurance. "Sure, if I could do a few things differently, I would, but God has given me peace. I have accepted my life as it is, all of it. I have forgiven myself for the things I regret. I am happy." What a powerful and peaceful place to land.

4. Forgive yourself.

Forgiveness is a release of debt. It means you don't owe any further. There is no revenge or further punishment sought. This applies when forgiving others, and also when forgiving yourself. Release the debt and the anger toward yourself that causes you to beat yourself up. Notice the ways in which you are punishing yourself and withholding good things, and stop it.

Humility is the gateway to self-forgiveness. Forgiving yourself requires the acceptance of your own imperfections, even perceived and false ones. And that takes the humility to accept yourself as an imperfect being who won't always get things right or live up to expectations. If you are going to take back your joy, forgiveness is not a step you can bypass.

Forgiveness is a release of bitterness and resentment, of the need for revenge and perpetual anger. It seems easier to understand these concepts when applied to forgiving others. When it comes to forgiving others, we are faced with three common myths of forgiveness:

- Forgiveness means what the other person did was okay.
- Forgiveness means the relationship has to stay the same.

- Forgiveness means giving up your right to feel hurt by the situation or express your negative emotions to the other person.

Now, consider what these myths look like when we apply them to ourselves. Remember that guilt is a form of self-anger. Anger is an emotion that tells us a boundary has been crossed. In the case of self-anger, you've crossed your own boundaries by not aligning your actions with the boundaries that are your values. If you forgive yourself for something that has caused authentic guilt, it does not mean what you did is okay. It means you choose to learn the lesson, pay the consequence, and change your behavior. Forgiveness of yourself is also an opportunity to become a better version of yourself. The relationship should not remain the same. Whether it is gaining the courage to have a tough conversation with a guilt tripper or making the decision to trust your instincts and ability to hear from God, forgiving yourself means growing yourself, not remaining the same. Use your guilt dilemma as an opportunity to evolve, to go to the next level, to be honest about your self-sabotaging habits and let them go. And lastly, when you forgive yourself, you choose self-compassion. You stop beating yourself up and instead decide to be gentle with yourself. You even acknowledge how hard this is. You speak to yourself the way you'd speak to someone you care about if they were struggling to forgive themselves.

In the same way that unforgiveness of those who have wronged you means holding on to the negative emotions you feel for them and the situation, unforgiveness of yourself also means you are holding on to negative emotions about yourself that it's time to release. Have you ever known a joyful person who is perpetually angry? If you want to take back your joy, forgive yourself.

5. Articulate your lessons.

Think about the guilt dilemma that has plagued you most. It may be the one you've overcome or feel yourself overcoming as a result of the words in this book. Now ask, *What is the most important message for me in this situation?* When you are able to put into words exactly what your challenge has taught you, you solidify new or expanded values that you truly own. There is peace in knowing what you believe and why.

Some lessons we can learn because others tells us, but the lessons we tend to embrace most are those we've learned through experience. Two of my biggest lessons when it comes to letting go of my guilt are lessons I shared a few pages ago, but I believe they bear repeating. As women, we can feel a lot of cultural pressure to conform to norms that may not be our own, but remember:

- Until you accept and embrace the unique life God created you for, you'll feel guilty for not living the life you think others expect of you.
- You cannot accept and embrace the unique life God created you for if you don't truly believe God created you for a purpose—a purpose that may look different from those around you.

Don't just casually ponder the message and lesson being offered to you. Articulate it clearly. Print it out. Keep it in front of you. It will bring you freedom. And with freedom comes joy.

6. Spend time with people who make you feel good, not guilty.

Some guilt trippers and manipulators are not as easy to set boundaries with as others. You might not want to cut your parent or child out of your life, but there are some relationships that simply don't hold that sort of weight in your life. If the boundary-setting conversations we've talked about don't work because the other person refuses to respect your boundaries, move on from the relationship. Then start intentionally seeking and nurturing healthy friendships with people who don't like guilt trips, people who celebrate with you and are authentic. These people should share your values so that you don't find yourself trying to live up to expectations and values that are not aligned with yours.

As simple as it sounds, surrounding yourself with people who make you feel good about yourself, people who make you laugh, and people you respect is a major key to joy. For the most part, we are as happy as our relationships, I once heard Pastor Andy Stanley say. And it's true. If you are serious about taking back your joy and letting go of guilt, be intentional about who you spend your time with. Research shows that having just one happy person in your network increases your chances of happiness by 10 percent.[1] Happiness is contagious. What do your closest friendships and relationships pass along to you? If the answer is guilt, doubt, or insecurity, it's time to make some changes. The choice is yours.

7. Do stuff that makes you feel guilt-free and happy.

Putting yourself around people who leave you feeling guilt-free and full of joy is one step. But another very important step is doing things that make you feel happy and guilt-free. What brings you joy? What makes you smile? What activities align so perfectly with your values that you feel fulfilled when you do them? I've observed that many of us talk and think in the abstract about our dreams and things we'd love to do, but we put those things off indefinitely. Take the time right now to identify some of the things you love to do that you haven't done in a while. Perhaps it's volunteer work. Perhaps it's a weekend getaway you've daydreamed about. Perhaps it's that 5K you keep thinking you can run, or maybe it's even something simple at home. Then do it! Whatever it is, start doing the kinds of things that make you feel good and that line up with your values.

Next, examine the things you're doing that don't line up with your values. Those things that leave you feeling guilty: A relationship you're hiding. The apology you have not given or accepted. The quiet time you want to spend praying or reading Scripture but you never actually do. What if, right now, you identified how much time you could dedicate, and then you just did it? It is often the things that have been hanging over our heads that weigh us down with guilt. So make a decision to stop procrastinating and hesitating, and do it. Even if it's hard. Even if you don't feel like it. Even if you're anxious about it. Remember, guilt is an opportunity to grow and push through the uncomfortable.

8. Study the happiness triggers.

Lastly, my research has led me to identify thirteen happiness triggers, which I discuss in detail in my book, *Happy Women Live Better: 13 Ways to Trigger Your Happiness Every Day*. Most people use the same happiness triggers over and over again out of habit. But knowing all thirteen of them can help you be very specific in doing things that will bring you joy, oftentimes almost immediately. Below I'll tell you what they are and give you a declaration you can make to affirm your commitment to incorporating it into your daily life.

ANTICIPATION: Having something to look forward to every day, every week, and every season of your life. If you don't have something to look forward to, create something. Make plans! They can be as simple as remembering that you're looking forward to your favorite show tonight and you're going to curl up on the sofa with your favorite blanket and popcorn, or as elaborate as planning for your dream vacation two years from now. Research shows you can get as much out of planning and anticipating as you get out of the experience itself.[2]

DECLARATION: *Every day, I make sure I have something to look forward to.*

GRATITUDE: Being thankful for what you have. Gratitude produces positive emotion that releases feel-good chemicals in the brain. You can multiply the effects of gratitude simply by reflecting on *why* you are grateful. So take a moment on a regular basis to think about what you're grateful for, even write it down, and then reflect on why it matters to you.

DECLARATION: *I focus more on what I have than what I don't.*

CONNECTION: Connection, quite simply, is love. It is those moments when you connect heart-to-heart with another.

DECLARATION: *I am fully present when I talk to people. I pause, I listen, I connect.*

SERVICE: Service is an attitude that puts others before yourself, leading you to make a positive difference in the world. The core purpose of your life is to serve. Service is about the ways we can positively impact others on any given day. Taking the focus off of ourselves actually makes us happier by putting our lives into perspective.

DECLARATION: *Every day, I do at least one thing to brighten someone else's day.*

PURPOSE: Your purpose is the unique way in which you use your gifts, talents, and experiences to serve and impact others. It answers the simple question, how are others' lives better because they cross paths with you? Life is not simply about finding happiness. God created you for a purpose and has divine assignments for you to accomplish. Your job is to learn what that purpose is and live it. Just remember this: while your purpose is unique to you, it isn't *about* you. Your purpose always serves others in some way.

DECLARATION: *God created me for a purpose, and I cannot fail at what I was created to do.*

MOVEMENT: Just twenty minutes of cardio will boost your mood for up to twenty-four hours.[3] This is one of the fastest ways to boost your happiness. Take a walk, do jumping jacks at your desk, play outside with the dog or kids. Get moving!

DECLARATION: *When I move, I feel good.*

PLAY: Doing things just for fun boosts your happiness. There are many pursuits in life at which you need to excel, but have something in your life that is for pure joy. Genuine play requires you to be fully in the moment, which allows you to relax and takes you out of multi-tasking mode.

DECLARATION: *I give myself permission to play and have fun.*

WINNING WORDS: Your words can trigger happiness or negativity. Be intentional about speaking positively. Drop words such as *should* that leave you feeling guilty, and remind yourself that you have choices.

DECLARATION: *Every day, I speak words of hope, peace, and love.*

FINANCIAL SAVVY: How you use your money can make you happier. Living below your means, giving, and buying experiences rather than things (dinner with friends versus a new pair of shoes) have been shown to boost joy.[4]

DECLARATION: *I aim to live on less than 75 percent of my income.*

SMILING: We think we smile because we are happy, which is true. But when we smile, even if we aren't particularly happy, it makes us *feel* happier. The muscles that contract when you smile trigger the release of serotonin and endorphins in the brain. So be intentional about smiling at others and even smiling for no reason.[5]

DECLARATION: *Every day, I find a way to smile, especially on bad days.*

RELAXATION: Taking time to do nothing, to rest, and to get plenty of sleep boosts your joy. So don't just value getting things done; value your downtime too.

DECLARATION: *I sleep. I rest. I embrace what is.*

FLOW: Flow is your ability to concentrate so intently on an activity that you become absolutely absorbed by it. It feels like time flies by. It is that point at which your abilities match the challenge in front of you, and you are in the zone. Do it often. It'll bring you joy.

DECLARATION: *I minimize interruptions so I can embrace the task at hand.*

SAVORING: Savoring is being fully present with all of your senses, noticing and feeling everything about the moment. It begins with slowing down, letting go of thoughts about the past and future, and appreciating what is right in front of you right now.

DECLARATION: *Every day, I stop and savor the moment.*

What to Do Next

THE GUILT-FREE, JOYFUL YOU

Imagine what your life might look and feel like when you are guilt-free. Something powerful happens when you put words to paper, especially when it comes to your vision of yourself. We have walked through many pages together, and as our journey together ends, I invite you to walk forward with a clear picture of what it looks and feels like to have false guilt replaced with authentic joy. The same research that shows that writing through challenges is powerful also tells us to imagine a "best possible future self" scenario is equally powerful.[6] So take fifteen minutes right now to imagine yourself guilt-free. I invite you to write about it in detail. Write in the present tense. Paint a vivid picture. See yourself kindly setting boundaries, boldly resetting expectations, and freely embracing the joy of being true to your purpose and divine assignments in life. Take a moment now to vividly describe the guilt-free you.

Conclusion

The Secret to Letting Go of Guilt for Good

It was a Tuesday around 5:30 p.m. when the last member of my team left our office, which is just three miles from my home. I stared out the window of the bright and inspiring little space I'd created for my business. I worked hard for many years to get to a point where I could call such a space my professional home, and I had intentionally settled on this location because I could picture myself writing here. The floor-to-ceiling windows give me a peaceful, picturesque view of the natural beauty of metro Atlanta. And by that I mean a view of trees. Lots and lots of them.

As I sat pondering the writing I'd planned for the next two hours, a family of four brown deer and a buck emerged from the thick brush between our building and the next. They strode gracefully into an open area of tall pine trees directly in front of my office window. Two of them froze as they stared at me across the distance, sizing up whether I was a threat. Then they ventured toward the pond on the other side of the golf-cart path that cuts through this suburban forest.

I took a deep breath and contemplated the work I had remaining. I don't normally stay late, but on this evening, I needed to write quite a bit more in order to get on track with completing a very important project—this book.

The quiet of an office nestled in the midst of such a scenic environment inspires my creativity. I can recall many days when that creativity unfortunately carried the weight of guilt on its back, burdening my mind when I most needed to focus. But on this night, I felt relaxed. I felt focused. I felt free to write to my heart's content.

What is this feeling? I pondered as I took a break. That's when it came to me. The feeling was joy—a joy I had often not felt in the past when I needed to work late. I had prepared for this evening, explained my deadline to my husband, and asked him to handle the weeknight hustle that comes with three school-aged kids—school pickups and extracurricular activities, dinner, homework, and bedtime. Meanwhile, I had stayed at the office to get done what I needed to. In the past, this had been a guilt trigger for me. So this moment was a realization that the trigger had lost its power. *You should be at home every single evening or you are not a good mom or wife* had been replaced with *Sometimes you will need to change your schedule to accommodate the reality of your work. You are blessed with a partner who 100 percent supports you. And you are an example of purpose and persistence for your children.* It wasn't just a mantra to be repeated. I was living it and feeling it—and it felt absolutely wonderful.

No guilt. No doubts. Just living in the peace and joy of choices I fully own because they reflect the values I hold dear.

My hope is that your journey has shifted your perspective too, helping you distinguish between authentic guilt and false guilt—and then let it go so you can take back the joy that is possible for your life. I invite you to revisit these concepts as often as you need to, and here's why: letting go of guilt isn't a one-time action step. It's a level of resilience you build over time, noticing your thoughts and taking control of the wayward ones before they take control of you. It is something you must practice again and again. Like a muscle, the more you work it, the stronger it gets over time. You'll be tested on a daily basis—when old thoughts and expectations sneakily creep in, when people close to you invite you on guilt trips, and when you fall short of your own expectations.

So remember these key points:

- Some days, you'll be better at letting go than others. That's okay. Don't beat yourself up. Just notice where you are and keep trying. Keep moving forward. Refuse to be discouraged. See it as progress when you catch yourself making decisions out of guilt, because it means you are labeling the emotion and pausing before allowing a fight-or-flight reaction to take over. Just remember: letting go of guilt is a decision only you can make.

- Letting go of the guilt is a choice—but it's not a one-time choice. If you set up the expectation that it's a one-time choice, then you're going to feel guilty about the fact that you haven't been able to let go of all your guilt. Instead, it is a choice you make over and over and over again. You must decide that no matter how many times you fall back into feeling guilty, you will make the choice once again to peel back the layers so that you can dismantle false guilt. Sis, stop right now and tell yourself that you'll make that decision again and again until guilt-free living becomes your new normal.

- Letting go of guilt takes practice, so keep practicing. The more you do it, the easier it becomes. Then, one day, you'll notice the weight has lifted. Your joy is back. Peace prevails.

- It will always be tempting to go back to what's safe. Don't forget that happiness is a risk. When you decide to focus on joy, fear may rear its head, pleading with you to stop dreaming a bigger dream for yourself. It is the Enemy's job to kill, steal, and destroy—and that includes your joy. Don't go back to the safety of dampening your joy by creating unnecessary guilt.

- Even when you own your values, you'll be constantly bombarded with influences to the contrary. You are surrounded by other people whose expectations will test you. Get comfortable standing by your values. Do what is meaningful to you. Line your expectations up with God's expectations, and peace will be your guide.

- Guilt has guided many of your decisions—and that's a good thing. Authentic guilt is there to help you align your values with your actions. This is a part of what makes you successful in life. People trust you. You want to do what is right. Having a conscience serves you well, and conscientiousness means you are diligent about meeting expectations. Just be careful about whose expectations you are diligent about living up to.

- The guilt trippers might not give up easily. If you deal with someone (or multiple someones) who has long used guilt trips to communicate with you, it may take more practice than you'd like to break this dynamic. Do not let this wear you down! Instead, wear them down by deactivating the buttons they've been pushing to get an automatic reaction. Set boundaries and stick with them. Soon, they'll go elsewhere with their guilt trips.

- Happiness takes practice. I told you this book is ultimately about your happiness. Guilt steals it. And when you let go of guilt, you make space for more joy. But it doesn't just happen; happiness is a habit. Use some of the happiness triggers to intentionally make daily choices to choose joy.

Thank you for allowing me to serve as your coach along the way. I'd love to hear how you've let go of the guilt, so drop me a line on social media. Tag me @valorieburton on Twitter, Instagram, or Facebook. I'm praying for you and rooting for you.

Love,

Valorie

Acknowledgments

I am so grateful for the committed and capable people in my life who support my work. I could not have written this alone, and I especially want to thank the following people:

My husband, Jeff. Your support and belief in me is unwavering. Thank you for being a sounding board for my ideas on this book and hanging in there with me through deadlines.

Sophie, Addie, and Alex, our children. I love you all and so appreciate your enthusiasm for my books.

Andrea Heinecke, my literary agent. Thank you for stretching me and believing wholeheartedly in my work.

Yvette Cook, my amazing friend for more than two decades. Thank you for brainstorming and listening and the assurance you gave me that the coaching process in this book works.

Meaghan Porter and Jenn McNeil, my editors. Thank you for your attention to detail and stretching me to make the manuscript the best it could be.

Leone Murray, my mom. You are my constant encourager and supporter. I am so blessed to get to work side by side with you for more than fifteen years now. I appreciate you so much.

Johnny Burton, my dad. Thanks for continuing to believe in me and my work, and for always serving as a wise sounding board when I need one.

Wade Murray, my brother. Thanks for your ongoing enthusiasm and support for my work.

LaChrissa Andrews, my assistant. Thank you for your servant's heart and beautiful attitude. You've made the writing process smoother, and I appreciate it.

Alexis Murray, my sister-in-love and coach training manager at The CaPP Institute. Thank you for your continual hard work.

I am blessed with many family members, friends, and colleagues who have chimed in on the guilt conversation with their experiences and insights. You know who you are. Thank you.

And to you, the reader. Thank you for the opportunity to share this message and walk alongside you on your journey to personal transformation. It is an honor.

Notes

Chapter 1: What Are You Feeling Guilty About?

1. *Cambridge Dictionary*, s.v. "guilt," https://dictionary.cambridge .org/dictionary/english/guilt.
2. *Merriam-Webster's Dictionary*, s.v. "guilt," https://www.merriam -webster.com/dictionary/guilt.
3. *Baker's Evangelical Dictionary of Biblical Theology*, ed. Walter A. Elwell, s.v. "guilt," https://www.biblestudytools.com/dictionaries /bakers-evangelical-dictionary/guilt.html.
4. *Baker's Evangelical Dictionary*, s.v. "guilt."
5. Interestingly, few modern English Bible translations use the word "trespasses" in Matthew 6:12, instead preferring "debts" or "sins." However, both the Anglican *Book of Common Prayer* (which drew upon Tyndale's translation of the Bible) and the traditional Catholic liturgy use "trespasses" in their renditions of the Lord's Prayer, and many English-speaking Christians may have memorized these versions rather than the direct quotes from Matthew 6. See *Encyclopaedia Britannica*, s.v., "Lord's Prayer," https://www.britannica.com/topic/Lords-Prayer, and Richard Beck, "'Forgive Us Our Trespasses.' Where'd That Come From?" *Experimental Theology* (blog), December 6, 2012, http:// experimentaltheology.blogspot.com/2012/12/forgive-us-our -trespasses-whered-that.html.
6. For more on cognitive behavioral therapy, see Martin E. P. Seligman, *Learned Optimism: How to Change Your Mind and Your Life* (New York: Vintage, 2006) and Karen Reivich and Andrew

Shatté, *The Resilience Factor: 7 Essential Skills for Overcoming Life's Inevitable Obstacles* (New York: Broadway, 2006).

7. Matthew D. Lieberman, Naomi I. Eisenberger, Molly J. Crockett, Sabrina M. Tom, Jennifer H. Pfeifer, and Baldwin M. Way, "Putting Feelings into Words: Affect Labeling Disrupts Amygdala Activity in Response to Affective Stimuli," *Psychological Science* 18, no. 5 (2007): 421–28.

8. J. David Creswell, Baldwin M. Way, Naomi I. Eisenberger, and Matthew D. Lieberman, "Neural Correlates of Dispositional Mindfulness During Affect Labeling," *Psychosomatic Medicine* 69, no. 6 (2007): 560–65.

9. Jared B. Torre and Matthew D. Lieberman, "Putting Feelings into Words: Affect Labeling as Implicit Emotion Regulation," *Emotion Review* 10, no. 2, (April 2018): 116–24, https://doi.org /10.1177/1754073917742706.

Chapter 2: Peel Back the Layers

1. "Cognitive Behavioral Therapy," Mayo Clinic, https://www .mayoclinic.org/tests-procedures/cognitive-behavioral-therapy /about/pac-20384610.

2. Laura A. King, "The Health Benefits of Writing About Life Goals," *Personality and Social Psychology Bulletin* 27, no. 7 (July 2001): 798–807, https://doi.org/10.1177/0146167201277003; Laura A. King and Kathi N. Miner, "Writing About the Perceived Benefits of Traumatic Events: Implications for Physical Health," *Personality and Social Psychology Bulletin* 26, no. 2 (February 200): 220–30, https://doi.org/10.1177/0146167200264008.

Chapter 3: Happiness Is a Risk, Guilt Is Safe

1. Brené Brown, *Daring Greatly: How the Courage to Be Vulnerable Transforms the Way We Live, Love, Parent, and Lead* (New York: Gotham, 2012).

2. Jill Jones, personal interview, August 29, 2019.

3. Jill Jones, personal interview.

4. Sonja Lyubomirsky, Laura King, and Ed Diener, "The Benefits of Frequent Positive Affect: Does Happiness Lead to Success?" *Psychological Bulletin* 131, no. 6 (2005): 803–55; Sonja Lyubomirsky, Kennon M. Sheldon, and David Schkade, "Pursuit of Happiness: The Architecture of Sustainable Change," *Review of General Psychology* 9, no. 2 (2005): 111–31.

Chapter 4: The Guilt Gender Gap

1. Frank Fujita, Ed Diener, and Ed Sandvik, "Gender Differences in Negative Affect and Well-Being: The Case for Emotional Intensity," *Journal of Personality and Social Psychology* 61, no. 3 (September 1991): 427–34.

2. Nita Lutwak and Joseph R. Ferrari, "Moral Affect and Cognitive Processes: Differentiating Shame from Guilt Among Men and Women," *Journal of Personality and Individual Differences* 21, no. 6 (December 1996): 891–96.

3. Brian Alexander, "Women Guilty of Feeling Too Guilty, Study Shows," NBCNews.com, March 11, 2010, http://www.nbcnews.com/id/35788411/ns/health-sexual_health/t/women-guilty-feeling-too-guilty-study-shows/#.XlmP5C2ZPPB.

4. June Price Tangney, Jeff Stuewig, and Debra J. Mashek, "Moral Emotions and Moral Behavior," *Annual Review of Psychology* 58 (January 2007), 345–72, https://doi.org/10.1146/annurev.psych.56.091103.070145; J. Haidt, "Elevation and the Positive Psychology of Morality," in Corey L. M. Keyes and Jonathan Haidt, eds., *Flourishing: Positive Psychology and the Life Well-Lived* (Washington, DC: American Psychological Association, 2003), 275–89.

5. Brett Roothman, Doret K. Kirsten, and Marié P. Wissing, "Gender Differences in Aspects of Psychological Well-Being," *South African Journal of Psychology* 33, no. 4 (2003): 212–18, https://doi.org/10.1177/008124630303300403; Fujita, Diener, and Sandvik, "Gender Differences."

6. Agneta H. Fischer, Mariska E. Kret, and Joost Broekens, "Gender

Differences in Emotion Perception and Self-Reported Emotional Intelligence: A Test of the Emotion Sensitivity Hypothesis," *PLOS ONE* 13, no 1 (2018), e0190712, https://doi.org/10.1371/journal .pone.0190712.

7. Itziar Etxebarria, M. José Ortiz, Susana Conejero, and Aitziber Pascual, "Intensity of Habitual Guilt in Men and Women: Differences in Interpersonal Sensitivity and the Tendency Towards Anxious-Aggressive Guilt," *Spanish Journal of Psychology* 12, no. 2 (2009): 540–54.

8. Jessica Bennett, "It's Not You, It's Science: How Perfectionism Holds Women Back," *Time*, April 22, 2014, https://time.com/70558 /its-not-you-its-science-how-perfectionism-holds-women-back/; Mary Ward, "Women More Likely to Be Perfectionists, Anxious at Work," *Sydney Morning Herald*, April 17, 2018, https://www.smh .com.au/lifestyle/health-and-wellness/women-more-likely-to-be -perfectionistic-anxious-at-work-20180412-p4z971.html.

9. Leslie P. Kamen and Martin E. P. Seligman, "Explanatory Style and Health," *Current Psychological Research and Reviews* 6, no. 3 (1987): 207–18, https://doi.org/10.1007/BF02686648.

10. Fatemeh Bahrami and Naser Yousefi, "Females Are More Anxious than Males: A Metacognitive Perspective," *Iranian Journal of Psychiatry and Behavioral Sciences* 5, no. 2 (Autumn–Winter 2011): 83–90.

11. Paul Glavin, Scott Schieman, and Sarah Reid, "Boundary-Spanning Work Demands and Their Consequences for Guilt and Psychological Distress," *Journal of Health and Social Behavior* 52, no. 1 (2011): 43–57, https://doi.org/10.1177/0022146510395023.

Chapter 6: The Upside of Guilt

1. Alex Korb, *The Upward Spiral: Using Neuroscience to Reverse the Course of Depression, One Small Change at a Time* (Oakland, CA: New Harbinger, 2015), 158–59.

2. Kirsten A. Passyn and Mita Sujan, "Self-Accountability Emotions and Fear Appeals: Motivating Behavior," *Journal of Consumer Research* 32, no. 4 (March 2006): 583–89, https://doi.org/10.1086/500488; Igor Knez

and Ola Nordhall, "Guilt as a Motivator for Moral Judgment: An Autobiographical Memory Study," *Frontiers in Psychology* 8 (May 2017): 750, https://doi.org/10.3389/fpsyg.2017.00750.

3. Francis J. Flynn and R. L. Schaumberg, "Clarifying the Link Between Job Satisfaction and Absenteeism: The Role of Guilt Proneness," *Journal of Applied Psychology*, vol. 102, no. 6 (June 2017): 982–92.

4. Francis J. Flynn, "Defend Your Research: Guilt-Ridden People Make Great Leaders," *Harvard Business Review,* January–February, 2011, https://hbr.org/2011/01/defend-your-research-guilt-ridden -people-make-great-leaders?autocomplete=true.

5. Gerard Matthews, Ian J. Deary, and Martha C. Whiteman, *Personality Traits*, 2nd ed. (Cambridge, UK: Cambridge University Press, 2003); S. Rothmann and E. P. Coetzer, "The Big Five Personality Dimensions and Job Performance," *SA Journal of Industrial Psychology* 29 (October 2003), https://doi.org/10.4102 /sajip.v29i1.88; B. W. Roberts and J. J. Jackson, "Sociogenomic Personality Psychology," *Journal of Personality* 76 (2008): 1523–44.

6. B. W. Roberts, J. J. Jackson, J. V. Fayard, G. W. Edmonds, and J. Meints, "Conscientiousness," in M. R. Leary and R. H. Hoyle, eds., *Handbook of Individual Differences in Social Behavior* (New York: Guilford Press, 2009), 369–81.

7. Lexico (Oxford Dictionary online), s.v. "conscientious," https:// www.lexico.com/definition/conscientious.

8. B. W. Roberts, K. E. Walton, and T. Bogg, "Conscientiousness and Health Across the Life Course," *Review of General Psychology* 9 (2005): 156–68.

9. Jennifer V. Fayard, Brent W. Roberts, Richard W. Robins, and David Watson, "Uncovering the Affective Core of Conscientiousness: The Role of Self-Conscious Emotions," *Journal of Personality* 80, no. 1 (2012): 1–32, https://doi.org/10.1111/j.1467–6494.2011.00720.x.

Chapter 7: (Re)Set Your Expectations

1. Oxford Dictionary, s.v. "should," https://www.oxforddictionaries .com/definition/english/should.

2. Reshma Saujani, "Teach Girls Bravery, not Perfection," TED, https://www.ted.com/talks/reshma_saujani_teach_girls_bravery _not_perfection/transcript?language=en.

3. Carol S. Dweck, *Mindset: The New Psychology of Success* (New York: Ballantine, 2008).

4. Tom Rath and James K. Harter, *Wellbeing: The Five Essential Elements* (New York: Gallup Press, 2014).

Chapter 8: Flip the Guilt Trip

1. Urban Dictionary, s.v. "Guilt trip," https://www.urbandictionary .com/define.php?term=Guilt%20trip.

2. Robert B. Cialdini, *Influence: Science and Practice* (New York: HarperCollins College, 1993).

Chapter 9: Take Back Your Joy

1. Harvard Medical School, "Happiness Is 'Infectious' in Network of Friends: Collective—Not Just Individual—Phenomenon," ScienceDaily, December 5, 2008, http://www.sciencedaily.com /releases/2008/12/081205094506.htm; James H. Fowler, Nicholas A. Christakis, "Dynamic Spread of Happiness in a Large Social Network: Longitudinal Analysis over 20 Years in the Framingham Heart Study," *British Medical Journal*, December 4, 2008, 337.

2. Jeroen Nawijn, Miquelle A. Marchand, Ruut Veenhoven, and Ad J. Vingerhoets, "Vacationers Happier, but Most not Happier After a Holiday," *Applied Research in Quality of Life* 5, no. 1 (2010): 35–47, https://doi.org/10.1007/s11482-009-9091-9.

3. Timothy W. Puetz, Sara S. Flowers, and Pat O'Connor, "A Randomized Controlled Trial of the Effect of Aerobic Exercise Training on Feelings of Energy and Fatigue in Sedentary Young Adults with Persistent Fatigue," *Psychotherapy and Psychosomatics* 77, no. 3 (2008):167–74, https://doi.org/10.1159/000116610.

4. Travis J. Carter and Thomas Gilovich, "I Am What I Do, Not What I Have: The Centrality of Experiential Purchases to the

Self-Concept," *Journal of Personality and Social Psychology* 102, no. 6 (2012), 1304–17, https://doi.org/10.1037/a0027407.

5. Paul Ekman, Richard J. Davidson, Wallace V. Friesen, "The Duchenne Smile: Emotional Expression and Brain Physiology II," *Journal of Personality and Social Psychology* 58, no. 2 (February 1990): 342–53.

6. Laura A. King, "The Health Benefits of Writing About Life Goals," *Personality and Social Psychology Bulletin* 27, no. 7 (2001), 798–807; Kennon M. Sheldon and Sonja Lyubomirsky, "How to Increase and Sustain Positive Emotion: The Effects of Expressing Gratitude and Visualizing Best Possible Selves," *Journal of Positive Psychology* 1, no. 2 (2006): 73–82.

About the Author

VALORIE BURTON helps readers find fulfillment and joy while navigating the challenges of modern life. She has written thirteen books on personal development and is founder of the Coaching and Positive Psychology (CaPP) Institute, which provides coaching, coach training, and resilience training and certification programs for individuals and organizations. Her unique combination of research, faith, and personal transparency inspires action and delivers practical tools for success in work and life. She and her husband grew up in Denver, Colorado, and live near Atlanta, Georgia, with their children. Get inspired with her videos, courses, and writing online at www.valorieburton.com and www.cappinstitute.com.

LEARN THE ART OF CHOOSING THE MEANINGFUL OVER THE URGENT.

Too many of us are living in time poverty, drowning in time debt, and missing out on the things that matter most. *It's About Time* unlocks an approach to life that Valorie Burton calls, "living time-lessly." You will come to understand

- the gradual changes that have led us to a place where having too much to do and too little time to do it is the norm,
- the vision for what it could be like if you were free from the stress of time and how to blast through the obstacles to those possibilities, and
- the practical steps to choosing the meaningful over the urgent so that your life is unhurried yet purposeful and reflects the values and impact that are unique to you.

AVAILABLE WHEREVER BOOKS AND EBOOKS ARE SOLD

This Is Where I Started

The subject of time is something I have wrestled with my entire life. I've always seemed to think I can get more done in a day than I can, leaving me with the feeling that I've never done enough. I've jokingly called myself a "recovering procrastinator," and the modern pull of digital distractions has made it easier than ever to put off the things that matter. Not to mention, my struggle with perfectionism has meant it's never quite the right time to get started anyway. Then I found myself racing against a biological clock in my thirties, afraid my life's most meaningful dream might pass me by altogether. Because my struggle with time has often felt like a stronghold, a thorn in my side I could not pluck out, I have desperately wanted to untangle its grip on my life. The day it came to me that I should write this book was pretty frustrating. I will share more about that in a moment, but let me encourage you that sometimes it is your frustration that fuels your turnaround. Sometimes you become so exasperated by the thought of continuing on the path you have been traveling that you suddenly feel the conviction to finally do whatever it takes to change. That is the place where this journey started. For years, I coached others to get unstuck, and now I needed to get myself unstuck.

I invite you to step through this journey with me, as I share timeless truths and practical steps that will open your eyes to the insidious nature of our problem with time. It is a problem that has evolved, slowly taking us further and further from nature's rhythm and moving us toward the unsustainable pace and load of a technology age. You, me, and millions of others struggle daily to keep up.

I knew deep down that the journey I embarked on was not just for me. It was meant to make its way onto the page to help you too. That thought was intimidating, but also motivating. The pressure and accountability of helping you ultimately helped me. My desire is for you to walk away from this book with an understanding of the eternal value of your finite time—and why and how you must intentionally choose the meaningful over the urgent every single day.

Our culture makes it so that even the most organized and efficient among us feels the pressure of the ticking clock and the possibility and regret of missing out. Modern life has evolved in a way that sets us up for stress, pressure, and overload. New norms and attitudes tap into deeply wired psychological impulses that make it harder than ever to take control of our time. Many of us also have one or more innate personality traits that make the struggle even worse. Perhaps you can relate to one or more of them:

- Optimism
- Perfectionism
- Overachieving
- Over-responsibility
- Approval addiction
- Misplaced guilt

No wonder time can become a tyrant that leaves you chronically stressed and discontented.

It would be enough if the ultimate consequences were only stress and discontentment. But those are just symptoms. Instead, it's the prospect of living a life in which you spend your time doing the things that *seem* important, only to look back and realize you missed out on the things that actually *are*. Today, this ultimate consequence is becoming the fate of more and more people. The natural pace and rhythm of life has been disrupted and replaced by historical and cultural shifts I will describe in the coming chapters—shifts that have created new habits that have become so common they are the new normal. These shifts make it easy to choose the things that feel normal (because everyone else is doing them) over the things that are natural (because they grow out of how you were created to function).

My guess is you chose this book because something about the title, the cover, or the description resonated with you. Or perhaps someone gave it to you because they sensed you need it. Whatever led you here, you will discover the ways in which the world has redefined what is normal and gain an understanding of how that personally impacts you daily. My hope is that you broaden your perspective and see your life in the greater context of our increasingly demanding world. I will help you reimagine the possibilities for a life that is meaningful, at a pace that is natural, with a load that is doable. Then I will equip you with the tools to bring that meaningful life to fruition.

Through these pages we will explore three key pieces of information that will help you unlock an approach to life that I call *living timelessly*:

1. The history and gradual changes that have led us to a place where having too much to do and too little time to do it is the norm
2. The vision for what it could be like if you were free from the stress of time and understood the obstacles you must blast through to enjoy the life you long for
3. The practical steps to choosing the meaningful over the urgent so that your life is unhurried yet purposeful, and reflects the values and the impact you want to make that are unique to you

Breaking Free of Old Habits in a New Season

My professional journey has been a long road. I self-published my first book after discovering my life purpose in 1999. I was clear. I was inspired. And I was determined to follow the purpose I knew in my spirit I was made for:

To create and enjoy a fulfilling, prosperous, and charitable life—and to inspire others to do the same.

I remember so clearly the day I stood in the "women's interest" book section of a Barnes & Noble bookstore during a trip to Seattle and had a flash of inspiration about that purpose. I remember writing that mission statement and staring at it as I sat in bed journaling in my little condo in Dallas, where I lived at the time. I remember the possibilities that danced through my imagination, filling me with hope and energy for my future. And I remember the quiet intensity of writing my first book in cursive on legal notepads, too intimidated by the blank computer screen to type it all out. I felt so connected to those words, as if they were coming to me and then through me. Sitting at the desk in my spare bedroom on weekends and weeknights, I wrote my career into existence and dreamed that it could one day become all that I hoped.

My life today is so much of what I had hoped for. Like you, I have fought to get where I am. And yet I believe there is so much more to come.

In order to pursue my purpose years ago, I learned to do a lot with very little. Because my previous career was in marketing and public relations, I was able to use those skills to build and manage my business while simultaneously producing the content—books, media, coaching, and speaking—that is the essence of the business. For the first seven years, I bootstrapped it. And once I got my footing, I never stopped bootstrapping it. An abiding fear of not having enough has often driven me to be really conservative about my financial commitments yet overzealous about my time commitments. The habit of being conservative has served me well, as has the willingness to work hard, but like any good thing, too much of it can become bondage.

Our Lives Are Full

Like yours, my life is full. I am sometimes stretched thin by my travel schedule, three kids, and a husband who is a commercial pilot and travels fourteen-plus days per month. You have your own set of demands: your work, your commute, your children's needs, school, debt that compels you to earn as much money as possible, and striving to get to the "next level," whatever that looks like. The fact that living with no breathing room has become the norm for a large segment of the population is a threat to our well-being and happiness. There is an undeniable connection between time and happiness.

Perhaps you have so much to be grateful for, yet little time to enjoy it fully. Maybe you find yourself reaching milestones, only to push the finish line out just a little farther—always another project, another goal, another level. And perhaps you have started to wonder, *When have I done enough?* It is an unfamiliar question in an achievement-driven world—but it is a question that intrigues the soul of anyone who wants to be truly happy and create breathing room to enjoy the life she has created.

The journey to a life in which I am happily married, have the privilege of being a mom and a bonus mom, do work I truly love, and have strong friendships to cherish took many years. As it finally came together, I awakened to the reality that time and happiness are intricately interconnected. Margin empowers happiness. It is breathing room—the soft cushion between your schedule and your limits. And in today's world we have less of it than ever.

If you'll allow me, I will share throughout these pages a little of my personal journey, the fun experiments that helped me—along with my husband, Jeff—change our lives, and my hope for how they could help you change yours.

Our Aha Moment

While I was stuck in the Phoenix airport for ten hours on a trip I wished I had said no to, I had an epiphany that became the catalyst for this book. I was sitting at a tiny little Mexican restaurant in the terminal with my good friend Yvette, who had traveled with me for a business event. While we were waiting for our food, I poured out my frustration to her.

"I've always crammed more into my schedule than is sane," I said, reflecting on my deeply ingrained habit. What I really wanted was some insight—an answer that could help me break the cycle. And Yvette, being the wise businesswoman and coach that she is, was just the person who might be able to deliver.

"When I think about it, I was always praised for doing things fast, being the first, the youngest," I pondered aloud. "I finished college at twenty, grad school at twenty-one, started a business at twenty-four, and wrote my first book by twenty-six. Getting to the finish line fast was my identity."

That's when Yvette posed a simple but profound question.

"And what has that gotten you?" she asked.

I took a deep breath and exhaled. I briefly revisited each of those seasons of my life as I contemplated what might be different had I not rushed through them but had instead traveled a little slower, savored a little longer.

My mind drew a blank on the answer to her question.

"What has it gotten me?" I repeated back to her. "I'm not sure it has gotten me much. Well, except more stress. I often missed out on the journey while I was trying to get to some self-imposed finish line. But the finish line was usually lonely, less exciting and not as happy as I'd imagined it would be." Overachievement had been such a driver for me because it indeed gave me something: approval and acceptance. That vulnerability led me to overcommit, and at times, overwork.

Have you ever had a moment where a thought so deeply resonated with you that you just had to sit with it to process it? This was one of those moments.

The cashier interrupted my thoughts when she called out that my food was ready. I went to the counter to get my quesadilla and then sat back down at the table with Yvette.

"I'm still that twentysomething young woman racing to a finish line that keeps getting pushed out. I have everything I thought I wanted in life—a loving, fun, supportive husband, children I feel uniquely called to raise, purposeful work, family within minutes from home. But I am doing too much. I want more time to savor it!" I lamented.

"Maybe your flight being delayed is a message," Yvette said with a chuckle. "You know God will sometimes stop us in our tracks to get our attention."

As if on cue, my phone started ringing. It was my husband, Jeff, FaceTiming to tell me he'd had an epiphany about our jam-packed lifestyle.

"You know how you're always talking about margin?" he asked, as though he'd been eavesdropping on the conversation.

"Yes," I said.

"I never really got what you were talking about," he admitted. "But I was sitting here meditating, and it occurred to me that I don't think I've had margin for at least ten years!"

Stunned, I had to stop and wrap my head around the first part of that last sentence: *I was sitting here meditating.* Jeff's faith is at his core; however, when I had suggested he spend time in quiet meditation, he'd brushed me off. But recently he'd decided to try it, and lo and behold, he got clarity about margin on the same day I was wrestling with the same issue!

Whenever a great speaking opportunity came along, I'd ask him, "Do you think I should do this? I mean, do you think this is good for our schedules?" And without hesitation, he'd *always* answer the same way: "Do it. That sounds great." It's in his nature to be supportive of my career, so his answer was always yes. But I was asking his opinion because I realized our schedules were already full and I needed help saying no. So this call was a *big deal*. On this day, in the middle of the airport, he called to say he finally got it.

"I don't know what we need to do differently, but we need to do something," he declared. It was our aha moment.

Experimenting with Change

Within a few weeks, we embarked on some experiments to see if we could get control of our time. Our goals were to create more meaningful experiences, make more time for each other and for our children, and decrease our stress. We called them "experiments" because we didn't want to make big declarations about what to change, only to discover we couldn't live up to them permanently or that they weren't having the impact we'd hoped for. Making these changes and activities into experiments felt doable, flexible, and, frankly, fun. If they worked, we'd keep them up. If they didn't, we could drop them or tweak them without feeling like we'd failed.

We began by simply talking about what we were feeling and what we wanted to feel instead. Summarizing how I felt was simple: I felt as though I were eating my favorite dessert, homemade strawberry cake, but I was being forced to eat it in record time with a stopwatch hovering over me, rather than savoring one piece at a time. In other words, my schedule had become so overloaded I couldn't enjoy the very things I love. Time with my husband and children always felt rushed or too short, and the work I am passionate about felt like an intrusion on my life. Jeff felt a lack of clarity about the impact of his schedule on our lives. For more than fourteen years, he's been a dad who flies an average of two weeks every month. When he's home, he's all here. But when gone, he's totally gone—sleeping in different cities nearly every night, wherever his last flight of the day happens to land.

So we each began with simple experiments. I reflected on my original life vision. I can still picture the day I pulled up to my apartment during my first semester of grad school in journalism. I had a flash of inspiration that day that I could have a family life and a professional life without climbing a corporate ladder if I used my writing gift to become an author. I didn't know what kind of author at the time, but with my lifelong passion for books, the thought excited me.

I had tucked that dream away all of these years, and now, as I pondered the idea of getting control of my time and happiness, the inspiration that came to me two decades ago returned. It dawned on me that I was living my vision, but I wasn't taking advantage of the purpose behind the vision: the flexibility to control my schedule. Instead, I was working as though I had to abide by a corporate work schedule—you know, the norm of an eight-to-five routine. But why? What was the point of being my own boss if my schedule didn't meet my needs and those of my family? So my first experiment was to create a new normal for my work schedule—one that gave me the breathing room I needed.

As a coach, I believe I find the best answers by asking powerful questions—or PQs, as I like to call them when I am training personal and executive coaches. PQs are one of my favorite coaching tools, and I'll share lots of them throughout this book.

I started with this one: What if I didn't have to work every day in order to get my work done?

Just asking the question was inspiring. *What if I worked every* other *day?* I pondered. Hmm. That might feel like breathing room. I was intrigued but apprehensive. Could I get my work done? Would I feel guilty because my team was still working every day? Would it hurt my business? I decided I wouldn't know unless I tried it. I committed to doing it for thirty days. After thirty days, I realized my fears were unfounded, so I continued the every-other-day schedule for an entire year. Two surprising things happened as a result.

First, compared to when I worked every day, I was *more* productive, not less. This schedule forced me to prioritize, so I cut some activities that were not particularly meaningful for the goals of the business. I became more selective about what meetings I could attend because there was limited time for them. And I was much more focused during my work days because I knew I had to get my work done or I could not take the following day off. It was built-in accountability.

Second, and amazingly, during the year when I worked less than I ever had in twenty years of business, we had our highest revenues to date. Taking time off didn't hurt the business; it seemed to have helped it. Not only was I more focused, but I was also more creative and happier. Time away from the office helped me gain perspective and see the big picture. And my team took ownership of projects in new ways, generating ideas and solutions to problems without my input. It felt as if I'd hit the jackpot.

At the same time, we did an experiment for Jeff to gain the clarity he wanted about his schedule. One evening after the kids went to bed, we pulled out the flip chart we used for family meetings, calculated how he spent his time in a typical month, and created a visual that I call a time chart. He had a black marker in his hand and a calculator.

Ever since that day in the Phoenix airport, when he told me he hadn't had breathing room in his life since becoming a parent more than a decade ago, he'd said he needed to make a time chart. I wasn't sure what he meant by that, but as I sank into the sofa, eyes fixed on the numbers he was writing on the large white sheets of paper, suddenly I got it. Jeff wanted to figure out how he was spending his life—or rather, his time. And he didn't like what he saw.

He took the schedule for that month and broke it down by work, sleep, family time, marriage time, commute time, and more. And as he calculated the numbers, we were flabbergasted. Here's what we estimated based on 720 hours in a thirty-day month:

TIME EXPENSE	ESTIMATED AMOUNT OF TIME SPENT IN HOURS	PERCENT OF TIME USED (BASED ON 720-HOUR MONTH)
Working as a pilot 14 days per month (traveling, flying, sleeping away from home)	336+	47
Sleeping at home	128	18
Transporting the girls to school, appointments, and extracurricular activities	54	8
Eating with and cooking for the family	32	6
Personal hygiene on days at home	10	1

Whoa. We sat on the sofa and stared at the numbers. Seeing the hours written on the flip chart made three things clear. First, his work took up nearly half of his life. The average full-time person spends about 197 hours per week (27 percent of their time) on work, including getting ready for work and commuting. But as an airline captain, Jeff doesn't come home when he's working, so he spent 336 hours per month away for work. That was 47 percent of his available time each month.

Second, he hadn't realized how much time he spent driving. Jeff has joint custody of two kids from his previous marriage, and they attend school about thirty minutes from our home. The girls have a joke that they drive to Alaska each school year (we travel about seven thousand miles a year going to and from school). At the time, one was in elementary school and the other was in middle school, so that meant an hour-and-a-half round trip to take them to school in the morning and more than two hours to pick them up, since their schools let out an hour apart. Plus, on some days they had extracurricular activities. As a parent, you gladly do what you have to do to raise your children. But seeing the hours on paper was eye-opening.

Third, after calculating five basic activities, we realized Jeff had just 20 percent of his time left to do everything else in his life—from working out and running errands to time with me and our three children, not to mention time with friends or leisure time. It became obvious that something needed to change.

Just these two simple experiments opened the door to change. The benefit of using experiments to clarify how to take control of your time is not unique to me and my family. I believe if you are willing to map out your own journey by trying small changes and building on them, you will see transformation, perhaps in unexpected ways. In fact, I think that time charts are so revealing, I'm going to ask you to create your own, even before you read chapter 1. (See "This Is How You Start.")

After we began these experiments, we started asking questions of ourselves:

- What are our true priorities, and how does the way we spend our time reflect those priorities?
- What stresses us most about the time challenges we face, and what do we control that could ease that stress?
- Looking into the future, what is our hope for the big change we'd like to see for ourselves and our family?

Our answers to these questions led to more small experiments that ultimately brought about big and unexpected changes in our work and personal lives. Here are a few of our small experiments:

- Jeff and I took once-a-month "staycations" in which we cleared the calendar for the day and spent that time doing something we both enjoy—going for a hike, getting a massage, or doing absolutely nothing at all.
- We left our phones at the front door for the first two hours after arriving home, rather than keeping them on us in the house.
- We tried flying together as a family to some of my speaking engagements. Doing so meant that rather than being away from home, "home" came with me, alleviating the stress of being apart. This required doing something Jeff had never done in eighteen years of flying: dropping trips from his schedule. This meant earning less money and making budget adjustments.

- When Jeff's company offered its pilots the unique opportunity to go on hiatus for a month, we jumped at the chance. He had a full month off, and we got to experience what daily life feels like when one person is not working.

As we put these experiments into practice, some healthy changes followed. We went as a family to speaking engagements in Florida, Texas, Ohio, New York, Pennsylvania, and even South Africa. Jeff gave up his nightly glasses of wine to de-stress and chose instead to exercise and pursue his own spiritual growth. We researched the idea of nontraditional schooling options for our son. We started talking about our dreams because we had time to just talk. In other words, we naturally began moving toward conversations and decisions that were meaningful rather than dealing with only the seemingly urgent matters of racing through our overloaded schedules. Margin gave us time to think and room to dream. And that's when something unexpected happened.

One day, while I was on the internet, a listing for a home appeared. To this day, I don't know where it came from. I don't remember if it was a social media post or an ad. But when I saw it, it reminded me of a dream my husband had shared with me before we got married. He had mentioned it while we were house hunting, and I had chuckled because it was so unusual. He told me that someday he wanted a house with an airstrip because his dream was to have his own small airplane.

"A house with an airstrip?" I had retorted with a laugh. "Where do you think we're going to find that?"

"Oh, they have neighborhoods where people share an airstrip," Jeff explained matter-of-factly. And then he drove me by one of the neighborhoods. *Who knew?* I thought and tucked the idea in the back of my mind for someday . . . someday way down the road. *Maybe.*

When I saw that house, I thought of his faraway dream and emailed the listing to him—not because I was thinking of moving but because I thought it would be neat to share it.

Unbeknownst to me, my husband began driving by that house a couple of times a week, daydreaming about the possibilities. Not only did the property have a shared airstrip, but it was also a horse farm. He grew up with horses and had worked on his family's dairy farm during the summers. It was his dream to have that life as an adult.

About six weeks passed before we decided to take an official look at the property. We were both reluctant. We had a plan, and it did not involve moving to a farm and having horses. But within minutes of stepping onto it, I felt a sense of peace. I remembered my own dream as a young adult of living in the country—but not too far from a big city—and having horses and land. It was a dream I'd buried long ago. As unplanned and different as this was from our home in a cul-de-sac in a subdivision with hundreds of houses, something about this just felt right. And so we went for it.

The process of writing this book led to experiments that opened up breathing room, which helped us rediscover our long-forgotten dreams and bring them to life. What occurred as a result came as a complete surprise and was quite the opposite of how I expected this journey to unfold.

As you begin on this journey, perhaps you'll discover your own beautiful surprises. You've landed on these pages with a hope, but what you receive instead might just be better than you imagined.